WHERE THERE'S HOPE

This Large Print Book carries the
Seal of Approval of N.A.V.H.

WHERE THERE'S HOPE

HEALING, MOVING FORWARD, AND NEVER GIVING UP

ELIZABETH SMART

THORNDIKE PRESS
A part of Gale, a Cengage Company

Farmington Hills, Mich • San Francisco • New York • Waterville, Maine
Meriden, Conn • Mason, Ohio • Chicago

Copyright © 2018 by Elizabeth Smart.
Thorndike Press, a part of Gale, a Cengage Company.

ALL RIGHTS RESERVED
This is a work of nonfiction. However, the author has changed the names of certain individuals to protect their privacy.
Thorndike Press® Large Print Basic.
The text of this Large Print edition is unabridged.
Other aspects of the book may vary from the original edition.
Set in 16 pt. Plantin.

LIBRARY OF CONGRESS CIP DATA ON FILE.
CATALOGUING IN PUBLICATION FOR THIS BOOK
IS AVAILABLE FROM THE LIBRARY OF CONGRESS.

ISBN-13: 978-1-4328-5048-7 (hardcover)

Published in 2018 by arrangement with Macmillan Publishing Group, LLC / St. Martin's Press

Printed in the United States of America
2 3 4 5 6 7 22 21 20 19 18

*This book is dedicated
to the safe return
of missing children everywhere.*

CONTENTS

7

PREFACE

As a little girl, I always imagined that I'd go to school, study music in college, get married, have a family, and be a music teacher out of my home. That was what I envisioned for myself, partly because that's what my parents envisioned for me, and I never dreamed that anything else could happen. I would grow up, find my Prince Charming, be a bride, and live happily ever after. I look around myself now and, yes, some of those things have come to pass, but when I was fourteen, I survived a horrific experience that forever changed my life and the lives of the people I love.

Afterward, I did go back to school and studied music in college. I married a wonderful Scottish man named Matthew Gilmour, an entrepreneur building a company in the vacation rental industry, and now we have a beautiful, vibrant little girl named Chloé. When she was born, she looked exactly like her father, with angelic, delicious facial features, and had a strong singing voice. My life has been and is filled with love and support. I am happy, but at the same time I'm dumbfounded at how different this life is compared to the life I imagined before I was kidnapped and brutally taught that "happily ever after" is a myth. Instead of quietly teaching music in my living room, I'm traveling almost constantly, doing everything I can to advocate for exploited women and children through the Elizabeth Smart Foundation and as a reporter at large for *Crime Watch Daily* and other news programs. I do quite a bit of public speaking, sharing my story and talking about what helped me survive and recover from this traumatic experience. I never asked for or wanted this platform, but it is what it is, so I'm determined to use it to help others.

I recently visited a small Ohio town that used to be a major hub of industry, with steel mills and automobile factories employing thousands of workers. Since almost all the factories have moved to Mexico or elsewhere, the population has significantly decreased. People go to where there are jobs, and the people left behind are struggling. At the venue, I was greeted by a flock of gracefully aging women. They brought me inside for the sound check, asked repeatedly if there was anything I needed, and told me how excited they all were that I was there. They could not have been more welcoming. It was like having an army of grandmothers looking after me. The auditorium held close to six hundred women, and I'm pretty sure I was the youngest one there by at least forty years.

After some announcements and housekeeping issues, the president of the ladies' group introduced me. "In 2002, when Elizabeth was fourteen years old, her story captured hearts and minds all over the world. She was abducted at knifepoint from her home by a pedophile and his wife. After nine months of indescribable abuse, she was rescued and returned home, thanks to the diligent efforts of her family and others who refused to give up the search. Sustained by faith, her family, and her own resilience, she rose above this ordeal and wrote about it in her bestselling memoir, *My Story.* She's now a wife and mother, an internationally recognized speaker, and an important voice advocating for exploited children and survivors of sexual violence."

It's always hard to hear my experience summed up this way. For eight years after I was rescued and returned home, I swore up and down that I never wanted to write about what had happened to me. I just wanted to leave it in the past. Then the criminals who abducted me were finally brought to trial, and I had to talk about it. But it just felt like facts on a piece of paper, and that felt wrong to me, because all those things happened, but that wasn't all that happened. My goal in writing my first book was to tell the rest of that story.

My goal when I stand in front of an audience is to let them know that they're not alone and that whatever they go through does not define who they are. So I stepped to the podium with that purpose in mind.

I smiled and said, "Thank you so much for having me here today. It truly is a pleasure to be here. I feel so lucky that I get to travel around the country and meet different people and work with different organizations. I've learned so much, but the one thing I have noticed that we all have in common is that we all have problems. We all have trials, and we all have those mornings when we just want to pull the covers back up over our head and go to sleep until all the problems disappear. Unfortunately, that never seems to work. At least not for me. But I've also noticed that every day, we make choices. And when we're faced with struggles, we have a choice to make: Either we surrender to our problems and give up, or we decide to keep moving forward no matter what. I'm not at all suggesting that once you make the choice to move forward, your problems disappear, but making that choice is the first step down that path. We are so often worried that we will be defined by what happens to us, and yes, that sometimes happens — when we let it. But it's important to remember that you are not defined by what happens to you. You are defined by the choices you make *after.* Some people will look at me and forever see the little fourteen-year-old girl who was kidnapped all those years ago, but when I look in the mirror, I see a wife, a mother, an advocate, a friend, a survivor — someone I want to be, someone I never want to disappoint. No matter what our situations may be, we always have the power to decide who we want to be."

After the speech, we moved on to a nearby banquet hall/restaurant for lunch and a Q&A session. A ninety-four-year-old lady seated at my table leaned over and said, "Dear, you did such a wonderful job, but I'm disappointed that you didn't speak more about God and his influence in your life."

"God certainly does play a big role in my life," I said, "but some things are a little more personal than others, and that is one of them."

I have always felt that this particular topic is a sensitive one. As a devout Mormon, I have a very strong faith, but I recognize that other people are equally devout in their own beliefs. I always want to be respectful and not give the impression that I'm shoving my faith down anyone's throat. Plus, I have always felt that my relationship with God is between God and me, something I treasure as very private. I don't want to sound as though I've sold my soul or cheapened my faith, and I definitely don't want to come off in a preachy way that might make others feel that I'm disrespecting their faith in any way.

This same lady happened to be the one saying the blessing over the food, and I have to admit, I was ready to eat. Exhaustion had set in, and I didn't want anyone to notice. Maybe it was because I was eleven weeks pregnant. Maybe it was the lack of a substantial breakfast or the time change from Mountain Standard to Eastern Standard Time. Two hours might not seem like a huge time difference, but at seven o'clock in the morning in Ohio, it is five A.M. in Utah, a time I'm not at my best. In fact, I'm usually flat on my back, mouth open, and snoring (or so Matthew tells me). That morning, I was functioning at a very low level of energy but trying to appear as if the exact opposite were true, and this sweet ninety-four-year-old woman got up and gave what felt like a twenty-minute prayer. Maybe that's not considered a long prayer to other people, but I wasn't sure if I was going to make it through.

When the prayer finally came to an end, I wolfed down the lunch that was put in front of me. (I would have had seconds if that had been an option.) Then it was time for the Q&A session. The wonderful thing about these senior ladies is that most of them aren't afraid to say what is on their mind. At the same time, the not so good thing about these ladies is that they're not afraid to say what is on their mind.

The questions progressed from "How did you meet you husband?" to "What happened to your captors?" Eventually one woman stood up and said, "I'm going to ask you an indelicate question. How did you not get pregnant during your captivity?"

This is not the first time I have been asked

that question, and she was absolutely right in saying that it is an indelicate one, something that really shouldn't be asked. There's no reason for it but idle curiosity, and while I'm willing to answer personal questions if it helps someone, some questions make me feel like I'm being tested, and I don't see any point to that.

I responded by saying, "Yes, wow, that is an indelicate question. I actually didn't start my period until I was fifteen — about three months before I was rescued — and those last three months . . . well, all I have to say is that it was a miracle that I didn't get pregnant."

The questions didn't go on too much longer after that, and I was grateful when the session came to an end. Afterward, I was approached by many of the attendees, who wanted to thank me and share their appreciation, which was so kind and sweet of them. Many of them wanted to take pictures with me, a request I always try to oblige, but when they took their smart-phones out of their purses, they realized that they didn't know how to work the cameras. I probably shouldn't be happy when that happens, but I was so drained, I wanted to skip for joy.

This type of event always leaves me wondering: *Did I serve a good purpose here today? What were the attendees expecting from me? What was I expecting from them? Was it worth a day away from home?* The questions I'm asked aren't always so pointed or personal. People are usually looking for some insight into their own life, not mine. They're hoping my experience holds some small piece of the map that will help them find their own way through whatever challenges life has handed them.

There's one question I get asked wherever I go: "Where does your hope and resilience come from?" The answer, for me, has three parts: my family, my faith, and a broad stubborn streak.

When I was a child, both my parents tried to instill in my siblings and me a determination never to give up, to always strive and hope for the best possible outcome. That mind-set influenced every aspect of our family life. My mother has always been my example in everything. I truly don't know where I'd be without her. Mom is and always has been one of my best friends, but she's also been my therapist, my teacher — everything to me at one point or another. Any time I would come home from school upset, my mom would sit me down, look at me, and say, "Are you going to let [insert bully's name here] choose your happiness?"

My mother was full of wise sayings and advice like that. I loved to horseback ride as a child, so whenever I hit a rough patch, she would say to me, "What do you do when a horse bucks you off?" And of course, we all know the answer: "Get back on." I secretly hated that, because she was continually making this decision to be happy my choice. It was my choice. I had the power to choose. As long as I was alive, I had the opportunity — maybe even the responsibility — to find a way to be happy. And in the end, it made a difference. I do have the power to choose.

As I travel throughout the country, I meet so many other survivors. So many people come forward and share their stories with me. I've seen that everyone has his or her own challenges to face, and as much as I or anyone else would like to know, understand, and help, it's not always possible to truly know exactly what a person is going through. Even two people who experience the same event will experience it differently, but on some level we all want the same things: love, happiness, and hope.

I don't think life is meant to be easy. We're challenged every day to see what we're capable of doing with this day we've been given, to see what choices we'll make, and ultimately, to see if the decisions we make will lead us to happiness. Even after I had accepted that "happily ever after" was a myth, I was not willing to accept that my fate was to live *un*happily ever after. I realized that I had been given a second chance at life. Everything — my family, my home, my chance to go to school — had been given back to me, and I didn't want to miss a second of living my own life.

What happened to me changed my life forever — not just that nine-month period, but everything that's happened to me since. I get asked the same questions over and over. Not about what happened so much as "How have you moved on?" "Have you forgiven these people?" "How have you healed?" "Are you angry?" "Do you deal with depression?" A lot of people are really struggling with these questions in relation to their own lives, and I can't even pretend I have all the answers. I've been searching for those answers myself. And seeking those answers — for myself and for you — is my goal in writing this book.

I decided to ask some of the people who inspire me how they rose above the challenges in their lives. Starting close to home, I interviewed my own parents, who'd faced every parent's darkest nightmare, and then I went out into the world and recorded conversations with a number of other people who'd survived extraordinary circumstances and were somehow able to get through it and go on to be happy and hopeful about life.

The challenges faced by these individuals transcend age, gender, religion, and geography. We all need to be reminded of hope. We need to believe that no matter what our situation may be, there is always a way forward. The more people I speak to, the more I realize that we all have a story to tell. In the following chapters, I'll take you with me to meet these people who graciously agreed to share personal stories that are astounding, inspiring, and sometimes shocking. Some of the people you'll meet are celebrities; some are everyday people just like you and me. Each of them has a unique perspective on moving forward and finding hope. They speak about grief, anger, forgiveness, relationships, love, faith, and finally achieving a baseline joy that makes life worth living despite its sometimes devastating challenges.

My hope is that through these conversations, you and I will both discover that we are all stronger than we imagined. We choose who we are, and happiness is within reach for each of us.

1
HOPE EMPOWERED

"Hope" is the thing with feathers —
That perches in the soul —
And sings the tune without the words —
And never stops — at all . . .
> — EMILY DICKINSON

*My mom will always love me, no matter what
has happened to me. My dad will always love
me. My siblings are stuck with me. No matter
what happens to me, my family will always
love me, and that is something that can never
be taken away from me.* That was my
thought the morning after I was kidnapped
from my bed at knifepoint and brought high
into the mountains behind my childhood
home.

I grew up in Salt Lake City, where my
family has been for generations. My father,
Ed Smart, was in real estate, and my
mother, Lois, was a homemaker. Right up
until the day I disappeared, I probably

would have said that there was nothing remarkable about my parents. They were just Mom and Dad, two kind, quiet-living, salt-of-the-earth people who were devoted to each other and to their children.

I come from a large family, the second of six kids. Although we all look alike — different variations of the same mold, fair-skinned and athletic — we are all different. But whenever we get together, there's teasing, laughing, and long conversations.

My brother Charles is the oldest and used to want everyone to know that, but he's also highly dedicated and fiercely loyal to those he loves.

I'm next, so for the first fourteen years of my life, teachers and kids in the school halls would always say, "You look just like your older brother!" (Ah, if only I were occasionally recognized now as Charles's sister instead of as "that girl who got kidnapped.")

Andrew follows me. Everyone likes Andrew. He is impossible not to like, making friends wherever he goes. When Andrew was a little boy, probably only about two years old, Mom had taken us shopping, and there was a lady standing outside the store smoking a cigarette. Without missing a beat, Andrew said to her, "Smoking is bad for you!" I think my mom died inside a little bit, and she quickly herded us into the store. When we were returning to the car with our groceries, the lady ran up to us and said to Andrew, "That was my last cigarette. I'll never smoke again." Whether it was his boyish charm or his sweet face, I don't know, but he got away with that sort of stunt then and still does now.

My only sister, Mary Katherine, is next. She is the kind of person who may seem quiet, even reserved, but once you gain her trust, you will have a loyal friend for life. We shared a room for almost our entire childhood. We were best pals. Being outnumbered two to one by boys, Mary Katherine and I had to stick together. Sometimes we would stay up late after our parents sent us to bed, just giggling until our dad would come in and tell us, "Girls, go to sleep. Now."

Edward is disciplined and serious. He's always known what he wanted and how to get it, and he has a million-dollar smile that tells you everything you need to know about him.

William is the baby of the family. Even though there are exactly eleven years and six days between us, we have always been close. When he was a little boy and would get scared at night, he would come into the room my sister and I shared and crawl into bed with us. I don't think Mary Katherine was too keen on that, but I would tell her, "One day he'll grow up, and he will never do this again, and then you'll miss it."

On June 4, 2002, I was fourteen years old, just about to graduate from junior high, and I couldn't wait to go to high school. I was sick of the dress code and riding the bus, and I was really looking forward to the alternating day class schedules. I was an intelligent kid, but I was very sheltered. Whenever I heard about kidnappings, rapes, or other crimes committed against people, I naïvely thought those things could never happen to me. They could happen to other people — people who lived on the wrong side of the tracks or made questionable decisions — but certainly never me. My innocence made my experience all the worse, because all the things that I thought could never happen to me did happen — along with a lot of things I could never have imagined happening to anyone at all.

In the early hours of that morning, I woke up with a sharp knife blade pressed up against my neck. A bearded man stood over me. He said, "I have a knife at your neck. Don't make a sound. Get up and come with me." This terrifying person dragged me out of my bed and steered me out of the house, threatening to kill my little sister if I didn't cooperate. I remember being led through my house and up into the mountains, praying every step of the way for an opportunity to escape, feeling scared that somehow I had missed that opportunity, sobbing, "Why? Why are you doing this?"

He said something about ransom. That I was his hostage. He told me to be quiet or he'd go back into my house and kill my family, and I believed him. He'd just demonstrated that he could do exactly that. He forced me to hike up into the trees a couple hundred yards down from the mountain ridgeline. There in the heart of the forest was a clearing. Part of the mountainside had been leveled out. On the south side of the camp, a retaining wall had been built up with branches and trees interwoven almost like a basket but not as tight. There was a large tent — maybe a six-person-sized tent. Tarps covered the ground around the tent and hung from the trees above, hiding the camp from view. I saw big plastic trunks, filled with I have no idea what. Behind the tent, there was a big hole in the ground, but it was mostly covered up with logs laid across the top and dirt thrown on top of the logs. A piece of skinny metal cable ran through the camp. It was tied around a tree on the west side and lashed to another tree on the east side.

A woman emerged from the tent. This image is seared into my memory. She was unlike any person I had ever seen before. She had long gray hair and hard, cold eyes that bored into me. She had a thickly built body and wore a long linen robe. She immediately embraced me in a very threatening way — like she was trying to tell me, *I'm in control. If you cross me, you'll be sorry.* She led me into the tent and sat me down on an upturned bucket. She brought in a small blue basin to give me a sponge bath. I was very shy, so I was appalled at the idea of anyone trying to undress me. Naïve as I was, I knew that this wasn't like my parents undressing me when I was a baby. Begging and pleading with her to leave me alone, I clutched my pajama buttons so they couldn't be undone and clamped my elbows tightly against my torso so she couldn't pull the top off over my head. Nothing swayed her determination to force me into a linen robe just like the one she had on. I did eventually end up in that accursed robe, but I finally convinced her to let me change myself. Later I realized what a big deal that was; I learned with brutal clarity that this was not a woman who was likely to adjust her chosen course. She studied me with those icy, calculating eyes as I changed, instructing me to remove my underwear, and then she scooped up all my clothing and walked out of the tent.

The man who had kidnapped me walked into the tent. He looked different. He had changed out of the dark sweatpants and sweatshirt he was wearing when he broke into our house. Now he wore a linen robe just like the one I had just been forced to put on, just like the one the woman wore. He knelt down next to me as I sat on the upturned bucket crying my soul out. I heard him speak, but frankly, I was in no state to understand anything he was saying.

No. Try. Focus, I told myself. *Find a way to escape. Find a way to call Mom and Dad.*

He would want to contact them. For the ransom. Then I could go home. I blinked hard and forced myself to hear what he was saying, but I heard only the last part.

"I seal you to me on this Earth, and I take you to be my wife. Before God and His angels as my witnesses."

I thought I had misheard. It was like a bomb had just exploded in my head. There was no way this was happening to me. *Seal you to me* — what did that even mean? I had only a shadow of an understanding. I had never even been on a date before, hadn't even had my first period yet. I wasn't an unintelligent girl, but I was oblivious to many parts of adult life, sex being one of them. I was mortified the whole time I had to sit through "maturation" class in fifth and sixth grade, and I conveniently managed to be sick during health class the day the *Miracle of Life* film was being shown. It would be accurate to say I was clueless about sex. And I should have been allowed to stay that way until I was ready to be otherwise.

I tried to reason with him, to tell him this wasn't okay, legal, or binding in any way. I tried to make him understand that this was wrong on every conceivable level — the list of reasons why went on forever. Of course, I understand now that reason had nothing to do with it. I'd never experienced any aspect of sex, but more to the point, I'd never experienced violence. I'd never been in a room with such soulless cruelty.

He pushed the robe up around my waist and forced me to the ground. Desperate to protect myself, I rolled away onto my stomach, because in my foggy idea of how sex worked on a mechanical level, I thought it had something to do with the two people facing each other. I thought it would be impossible if I were facedown with my legs crossed and clenched together.

There aren't words to describe the humiliation, pain, and total degradation I felt over the subsequent hours. I've learned and grown so much since then, but I still can't imagine anything worse. In my opinion, rape is worse than murder. The rape of a child is beyond the definition of despicable. When it was over, he stood up and walked out of the tent without the slightest shadow of regret. No concern. No remorse. No guilt over how he had physically damaged and emotionally destroyed me. I lay curled up in the fetal position on the ground. I lost consciousness. I must have been in a severe state of shock. Sleep was the only escape from the heartache and agony I was suffering.

I didn't know their real names at that time, but as I write this, from this moment forward, I intend to use the names of the people who kidnapped me: Brian David Mitchell and Wanda Barzee. I choose to do this, but not because I want to humanize them in any way. In the immortal words of J. K. Rowling, through the character of Dumbledore instructing Harry Potter to call his archenemy, Lord Voldemort, by his name: "Always use the proper name for things. Fear of a name increases fear of the thing itself." I refuse to ever again grant Mitchell or Barzee any power over my life or allow them to cause fear in my heart.

My next memory is of Mitchell kneeling over me. I was aware of his looming presence, but I didn't want to open my eyes. I was terrified he would rape me again. I hoped that maybe if I lay there not moving, he might leave me alone a little longer. But feigning sleep wasn't going to deter him. I opened my eyes, and there he was, as horrifying in real life as in my imagination, staring right back at me, running a length of metal cable through his hands. I promised that I wouldn't run away if he would just leave me free of physical bonds. That was a bald-faced lie, and he must have known it. From the instant I was brought into the hidden camp, I was looking for a way to escape, planning to make a run for it as soon as he and his real wife were asleep that night. Mitchell just looked at me, smiled, and said he was going to chain me up anyway. He said he was doing me a favor by removing temptation.

Mitchell left me in the tent, and though it was a bright, sunny morning outside, I couldn't have felt more darkness and paralyzing fear inside, shackled like a slave, brutalized, terrified. Alone and brought low — lower than I would have thought possible.

And that's when I had this one pinprick of hope.

My mom will always love me, no matter what has happened to me. My dad will always love me. My siblings are stuck with me. No matter what happens to me, my family will always love me, and that is something that can never be taken away from me.

The more I focused on this tiny shaft of light, the stronger and brighter it became, until I finally found that I had made a decision: No matter what lay ahead of me, no matter how many different tortures my captors thought up, no matter how long I had to live to outlive them, I was going to do it. I was going to do whatever I had to do to survive. Whatever it was, if it meant that somehow I would survive another day, I would do it. Because my family's love was worth it, and no one could ever change that.

That was my hope. That is why I survived nine long months of a nightmare. Every time I thought I had hit rock bottom, that I could sink no lower, these people would think up a new torture, a new way to destroy the minute pieces that were my shattered soul. But I made myself remember that I had something to hold on to, something to survive for, something that could never be taken away from me. I had this small, precious kernel of hope. I knew that I would always belong to a family, even if death separated us, and I knew that they would always love and accept me.

That hope is what sustained me through my darkest moments. I would have given up without that hope. I wouldn't be here today without that hope.

Hope, I've learned over the years and through my experiences, can be many things, ranging from wishful thinking — like "I hope it rains diamonds from the sky" — to something much stronger. It can outlast any darkness when it's anchored in truth, and that's what I experienced. We see it all the time in movies, books, and the news: how the human spirit can overcome unbelievable trials and adversity because of one simple hope. To me, hope is what gets us through everyday life, through our struggles, and our belief in hope is strengthened as we succeed or successfully overcome. I think hope is something we can create for ourselves, and it can be a stronger force than anything life throws at us.

■ ■ ■ ■

I know the basic facts from my mother's point of view, but I want to hear her thoughts about what she went through when her child was kidnapped and how she's processed it all during the years since it happened. I don't want to interrogate her — she's had enough of that — but I want to delve deeper than we have in the quiet conversations we've had in the past. In those conversations, we shied away from the difficult questions, and if I am to seriously accomplish what I've set out to accomplish in these interviews, I can't shy away from hard questions or avert my eyes from painful answers — not with any of the people I plan to interview, but especially not with Mom.

Sitting with her in the bright sunshine on the deck behind my house, I set my phone on the table between us and set it to record the conversation. Chloé walks between us, stopping occasionally to pat Mom's knee. Looking at her, all pigtailed innocence, it's hard to imagine darkness in the world. It's hard to imagine darkness in my own life. Her chubby little arms reach, trying to pull herself up onto the outdoor sofa in between my mom and me. It's easy to just watch her and forget about the reason I asked my mom to speak with me today. Mom probably wouldn't mind if we did. But I set out to do this.

"What happened the night I was kidnapped?"

"That evening was busy and happy," she says. "Like most evenings."

That's how I remember it, too, even though Mom had been going through a very difficult time. Her father had been diagnosed with a brain tumor three months earlier and died just a few days before I was kidnapped. Mom is as solid as the Rock of Gibraltar, but she was still reeling a bit from weeks of intense caregiving and worry, followed by the terrible loss of her father and then trying to help in any way she could for his funeral, which took place the day before I was kidnapped.

"After that," she says, "I remember thinking to myself, *I have to regroup and get things organized again.* I thought, *I'm going to plan meals better, and I'm going to be better organized and get back into the routine of things rather than flying by the seat of my pants.*"

That night, there was an awards ceremony for my eighth-grade graduation, and I was going to be playing my harp. I'd recently made the high school track team, so I wanted to go running before the ceremony. Mom didn't want me to go alone. She made me take my sister, Mary Katherine.

Mom says, "I was cooking dinner, thinking, *This'll be great. We'll have dinner and then run down to the awards ceremony assembly. Everything will be good.* You were late coming home from running, so that pushed dinner off, and I think your dad was even late coming home from work. I burned dinner, so I opened the kitchen window to air out the kitchen, ready to go to plan 2, which was to skip dinner and go straight to the assembly."

We left the house in a big, happy whirlwind, taking two cars because one car was full of children and the other carried my harp. No one thought anything of the open window, because Mom was always careful about things like that.

"I get that from my father," she says now. "He was very protective and conscientious about locking doors and making sure lights were turned off or the oven was turned off or the iron unplugged. Check the doors when you go. Check windows and make sure things are turned off and everyone is safe. But we left the window open, because there was a nice breeze coming down the canyon that would go through our home and cool things off, and this window was a tall, narrow window that you would think a child could get through, but not a grown man. When we were building our home, we were having the air-conditioning units installed and initially they were installed right below our kitchen windows, but I told Ed [my father] that I did not want those installed below the kitchen windows. Someone could get in. So after they were basically finished with installing the units — much to the workers' chagrin — I made them pour a whole new slab of concrete far away from those kitchen windows for the very reason that I didn't want anybody ever climbing in through those windows. After we returned home from the awards assembly, we went to bed, and Mitchell came in the early hours of the morning."

Hours later, Mary Katherine came into Mom and Dad's bedroom. She had her favorite blanket wrapped around her shoulders and draped up around her head. Mom described her as a frightened little bunny rabbit.

Mary Katherine said, "Elizabeth is gone."

Mom and Dad heard what my little sister had said but thought maybe she had been dreaming and that I probably had just gone to find another place to sleep because I had been kicked one time too many times or was too warm. (At that time, Mary Katherine and I shared not only a room but a bed as well.) Dad got up and started going from bedroom to bedroom.

My sister spoke again. "You won't find her. A man came and took her."

Now both my parents were frantically looking for me. They went downstairs to the kitchen. Mom slammed her hand against the kitchen wall switch, immediately lighting up the room. Her eye instantly went to a slashed screen above the kitchen counter. She knew that I was gone. Pandemonium broke out. My mom yelled to my dad, "Ed! Call 911!" And that was the beginning of a hellish nine-month nightmare.

"Those were hard days," Mom says. She can be the Queen of Understatement, always practical, keeping drama to a minimum. "I suffered — in a different way than you did, of course — but I know that if I hadn't had William, who was only three at that time, I could have gone into a serious depression. I would have never been able to get out of bed had it not been for him. He would come up in the morning and say, 'Come on, Mom. Let's go eat.' 'I need this.' 'Can you play with me?' Even though my mind was always on you, I had five other children I had to take care of. I was responsible for them. I couldn't project my feelings upon them, because they were back in school, and we were trying to make our lives as normal as possible. I couldn't give in to that worry — because they all worried in their own way. They all knew what was going on."

Now that I have my own little girl, I sometimes wonder if in some ways it was harder for my mom than it was for me to survive and keep going. I always knew that my parents loved me unconditionally, but now that I am a mother myself, I realize what it means to love someone unconditionally. And it would kill me if anything ever happened to Chloé. I think I would definitely fall into a deep depression with very little hope of ever coming out of it. So yes, William was, in my mind, Mom's salvation while I was missing.

"We never watched the television," she says. "We never really went out in public. We were very cloistered, away from the world and the media camped outside our home. We had the FBI live in our home for two weeks. They had these big booms, microphones they would raise way up tall to hear anything that was happening in the house. Helicopters would swoop down low, trying to get photos of us and the family. One time, I asked Mary Katherine to run out and get the mail, and in the news the next day, there was a picture of her running out to get the mail."

Mom is quiet for a minute or two, her eyes roving the hills beyond my backyard.

"The nights were the hardest and the longest. During morning hours, of course, the children would be up, and I'd have to continue on. I'll tell you, it seems like I didn't sleep for nine months, because at night, my mind would race, thinking, *Where is she? What's happened to her? Who has her? Will we ever see her again?* I had to be brought back to what I'd been taught growing up, learning from my grandmother and my mother and these strong women. I thought, *I can do this. If I don't have her here in this life, our beliefs are that she will always be my daughter.* I had the privilege of carrying you for nine months, right below my heart. Now it felt like my heart had been ripped out. But you would always be mine."

She knew that she had to be strong enough to care for me if I came home, and strong enough to care for my brothers and sister if I didn't. Hope was hard to find. My parents had been informed that if an abducted child

41

is not found within forty-eight hours, that child is most likely dead.

"I had nine months to think of that," says Mom. "We belonged to that infamous group of parents who had lost children — whose children had been kidnapped. Frankly, there weren't any happy stories. I never heard of a happy story from any of them."

But there were other stories. Mom and Dad began to hear from people all around the world who were praying for me, searching for me.

Mom says, "I don't know why, but the community — really, it felt like the world — got behind us and expressed their sympathy and told us stories about how they were looking in every vacant lot and shed, checking up on people and going everywhere. And to see the search go on for weeks and months . . . They never let it die. That was so faith-promoting for me. We were just an ordinary family. Nothing special to the world. They were special to me. Someone told me this was the biggest story of a kidnapped child since the Lindbergh baby — not that this brought comfort to me, but in a way, it was like you were everybody's child. I found some peace in knowing that everyone was out there looking for you. There were so many kind, good people."

As that crucial forty-eight hours stretched to forty-eight days, weeks turned to months, and the entire summer went by, Mom forced herself through each day.

"When school started, I couldn't look for clothes for Mary Katherine without thinking of you or wanting to buy you a dress. I went and bought your school clothes and shoes and had it all in your room waiting for you, because I knew you were coming back. Then Christmas came, and you weren't back. I couldn't do it anymore. I couldn't go out. It was hard talking to people. As kind and as good as they were, it was hard. I couldn't even bear to go to a store to even look for Christmas gifts for our family. It was like, 'We love you, children, and we want you to be happy, but . . .' I couldn't do it, because I was a mess," Mom admits, her voice full of emotion. "But on Christmas morning — and I don't know who did it to this day — there was a mountain of gifts on our front porch for all the children. It was probably the best Christmas they ever had. I was so thankful that somebody, or many people, got together and did that for us. Something I just couldn't do at the moment."

I'm so grateful to whoever it was that performed that great act of kindness. When

I returned home, I was completely over-whelmed by the love and support that the community showed us. I received boxes of mail. Our house turned into a florist shop with flowers on every table, including the bathroom countertops. There were so many thousands of people praying for us and rejoicing in our reunion that, although I was completely overwhelmed by all the atten-tion, I think I understand what Mom meant when she said, "It brought comfort to me that, in a way, you were everyone's child, and everybody was looking for you. I found peace in that knowledge."

Kindness, love, support, prayer — it all makes a difference. It made a difference for my mom while I was kidnapped, and it made a huge difference for me when I was rescued and brought home, to know that I wasn't an outcast or someone to be shunned for what had happened to me. It's a bit miraculous, isn't it? That people who don't even know you can make — and are mak-ing — such a difference in your life. Every time there is a natural disaster, a terrorist attack, or some kind of major accident, just think how many people immediately begin to pray, to care and wish for a positive outcome. All of that builds and strengthens hope — if we choose hope. But that can be a very hard choice sometimes. Like the choice to get out of bed when every moment of the day is agony. The choice to make toast for your hungry preschooler when your life and soul are in ruins and you don't even want to open your eyes, much less open your heart. That's when the kindness of a stranger or loving support from a friend can make all the difference.

Back when I thought I might resume my original plan for my life — to be a musician and a mother — I jumped at every opportunity to put my name out there as a harpist. As a teenager, I was thrilled at any opportunity to get paid for playing my harp, so I readily accepted when a friend of a friend asked if I would provide the background music at a fund-raising dinner at a beautiful restaurant in Millcreek Canyon, not far from my home. Ann Romney was there. (This was years before her husband, Mitt, ran for president; he was governor of Massachusetts at the time.) I don't remember if I even spoke to her that night, but I noticed her, and since then, I've admired her from afar.

Candidly, I love it when the Romney family attends our church, because they draw so much attention, hardly anyone notices me. It's not that I don't appreciate what people have done for me — I do, and I always will — but I also like to feel like a normal person and just sit in church with Matthew and Chloé and listen without overhearing whispers. *Yes, that's the girl who was kidnapped.* The Romneys have the process of entering and exiting the church building down to an art. They must have a countdown set on their watches, because they walk in and sit down as the first chords of the organ music play, and it's like a magic act the way they get out of there. I would love to learn the trick to making a quick yet completely gracious exit.

When I wrote Ann's name on my list of potential interview subjects, I had no idea if she'd have the time or if she'd even remember me, but I summoned the courage to ask, and she invited me to give her a call.

"Hang on one second," she says when she picks up the phone. "We're up at the lake. I found a quiet corner, but sometimes people find me."

"I know the feeling."

We spend a little time on small talk while she gets settled. I use the time to summon my courage and consult my notes. Having done my homework before the call, I know that Ann has been coping with the devastating effects of multiple sclerosis since 1998. I don't want to overstep what's polite, but I need to know, so I ask her, "When you found out you had MS, did you have anger about it?"

"I think I went through pretty much the stages of grief that people go through when they lose a loved one," she says, and for the first time it occurs to me that sometimes the lost loved one is yourself. "Anger is one of those stages. Denial was one. Boy, that was there!" She laughs a little at that. "Denial was strong. I'm like, *This is impossible! I cannot believe this!* Yet I'd wake up and I'd have these complete MS symptoms — numbness, weakness, fatigue, loss of the use of my right leg. It's like, *Yeah, what were you thinking? Of course that's what you have. You have the MRI imaging that shows the sclerosis on your spine. What else do you think it is?* But I did go through anger. It wasn't fair that I was not going to have . . . that my life was going to be different, or my life was over, and I was ruined, and I was never going to have another good day. I was angry. Thinking that, I moved into an eighty-year-old body and could hardly get out of bed. I couldn't help my family anymore. I couldn't do anything for anybody anymore. I could barely take care of myself."

She pauses, and I wait. I feel her considering what she wants to say next.

"I think everybody stays at different stages for a longer or shorter time, depending on what you finally decide you're going to do," says Ann. "I finally decided, *Well, this is my life. These are the cards I've been dealt. I better just live the best I can with what's been dealt to me.* That's where I think I started to say, *Okay, now what can I do to fight this a little bit? This is not acceptable to me. This is not my choice to live this way, so what can I do to make myself feel better?* That's when I started finding alternative strategies and different things. It took me a long time to get there. It took me about a year to get to the point where I was willing to say, 'Okay, I'm going to fight it, and I'm going to learn how to deal with this the best I can.' "

Ultimately, that's what it comes down to. We have a choice to make every day: Are we going to allow our problems to overwhelm us or are we going to move forward?

I love Ann for being so honest and sincere, for openly admitting that she went through a whole array of negative feelings. For taking the time to acknowledge what she felt and finally accepting it, but not just accepting it lying down. She takes a courageous stance, exploring every avenue to make small steps forward. I know it's easy to become overwhelmed; we all do sometimes, especially if we place so much pressure on ourselves to "get better" or "just get over it" or "move on." In reality, it's the small steps that take us the farthest. Ann Romney is a great example of exactly that.

"So much of the rebuilding that I did came from my faith and my belief that there was a better way," Ann says. "That there was going to be a better life. That there was going to be peace and strength again. It wasn't like I was — *boom* — healed. I went through a healing *process* where I was able to rebuild my life and rebuild my strength."

Today Ann Romney is back in the saddle, literally and figuratively. Our conversation takes a welcome turn to a topic we both love: horses.

"I'm riding like crazy, and I'm competing," she says. "The last horse show, I actually beat a couple of Olympians. Talk about feeling powerful! I never, ever, ever thought I would go down this way. It is the biggest kick in the pants, and I'm just loving it. I keep getting better, and I keep fighting and getting stronger. My horses are my partners. They're my buddies. I love them to death, and they really brought me through a hard time. Get me in the saddle, and my heart sings."

This strikes me as a great metaphor: *Get me in the saddle, and my heart sings.* But before I can say that, Ann says, "I have questions for you."

"Oh. Okay. I'd be happy to answer. If I can."

"What made you decide to write about this?"

"Well . . . whenever I say I'm not going to do something, I always end up doing it. I should probably just stop saying it."

I tell her a little about this quest I'm on: to ask the people who inspire me the questions other people always ask me, to find the answers for myself and then share those answers with others.

"Harold B. Lee, the great educator and LDS president, was a friend of Mitt's mother," says Ann. "She had a lot of health issues and was going blind at the end of her life. He said to her something which I have never forgotten. He said, 'Only the wounded can fight in the Lord's army.' I thought . . . wow. Only the wounded. Only those who've been through the breaking of the heart, and then the opening of the heart, and then the transformation of the heart, which then makes you more powerful."

The vivid image strikes me: the breaking and opening and transformation of a human heart. But then I wonder — though I don't disagree with the idea that you don't know how strong you are until you've been tested — haven't we all been through something? Aren't we all wounded in some way? I'm certain that we are, and I hate comparisons that make one person's pain outweigh another. Who gets the biggest tragedy award — the kidnapping victim or the cancer patient?

"There's nothing more painful than thinking that your child is being mistreated," Ann says with genuine empathy. "Your parents must have such extraordinary strength with what they went through."

They did — and they still do — but it can't be a competition if we truly have compassion for others and for ourselves. Life has a way of teaching us that lesson, whether we want to learn it or not.

"These experiences," Ann says, "they completely humble you. They break you down. They basically smash you to pieces. Then you have to start figuring out how to rebuild the pieces, and you do it through hope."

"Do you believe in happily ever after?" I ask. "In this life, I mean."

I expect her to confirm my conclusion that "happily ever after" is a myth, but without hesitation, Ann says, "You can have happily ever after in this life. But no one is going to escape this life without pain or suffering. I call it gathering our bags of rocks. Basically, as we go through life, we have our bag we carry over our shoulder, and each painful thing we go through in life — we just keep throwing more rocks in our bag. Oftentimes, other people don't see the bag of rocks we're carrying, but all of us will accumulate our bags of rocks."

I agree with her, but later in the day, contemplating our conversation, I decide that it's important to stop every once in a while, set the bag down, examine the contents, and leave some of those rocks behind. Otherwise, we might find that we don't have the energy to make it to our destination.

The day after I was rescued by police officers in Salt Lake City, I flew in an FBI helicopter over the camp where my captors had chained, raped, and tortured me. During those long, agonizing months, my deepest prayer, my most fervent hope, was that I would somehow be able to fly away from there. I watched and waited for an opportunity, praying that someone would help me. I remember a few times when helicopters were so close overhead that the wind from their blades beat down on the tent, making it shake. On those occasions, Mitchell would grab me and pull me into the tent lickety-split, and once Barzee was in the tent as well, he would zip the tent door shut and hold me in an iron grip. The helicopters never stopped for long; soon they were gone, soaring upward. The wind would die down, the tent would stop shaking, and my heart would once again feel like it had stopped beating.

That day nine months after Mitchell put a knife to my throat and took me from my home, there I was, looking down on the no-longer-hidden camp, surrounded by FBI agents and my mom. I went there again a week later with my parents. We hiked up the three and a half miles from our home. I wanted to take them there, because the most important thing to Mitchell was that this place be kept secret. He said it was a "sacred" place where he had thought up most of what he called his "revelation from God" or "divine inspiration" — which, in truth, were torture and foulness. Only someone who'd lost all compassion and human kindness could have thought those things up.

Standing there with my mom and dad, I

felt triumphant. Mitchell would spend the rest of his natural existence in a hell of his own making, but I was standing under the blue Utah sky, and his dark secret was laid open, exposed to the bright sunlight. The shroud of secrecy had been stripped away and could no longer harbor all the abhorrent details of what these people had done to me. Returning to the hidden camp, I faced the terrible memory of what had taken place there, but I also realized that it wasn't the mountain, trees, or plants that had hurt me, and now they were all that remained. My small, precious kernel of hope had outlived everything my captors could do to take it from me.

South African human rights activist Archbishop Desmond Tutu wrote, "Hope is being able to see that there is light despite all of the darkness." Hope is real. And it holds great power. Each one of us has the capacity to hope, but there are moments when we must ask ourselves:

What is the unique anatomy of my hope, and where do I find it?

How do I harness the power of my own hope and keep it alive as I move my life forward?

2
FORWARD AT ALL COSTS — NEVER RETREAT

Do not go gentle into that good night . . .
Rage, rage against the dying of the light.
— DYLAN THOMAS

Sometimes the struggle to survive within the human race is a visceral, physical fight for life. Sometimes it's not that obvious. It's not the knife wound or black eye. It's what's going on behind the perfectly coiffed hair and wrinkle-free attire. Survival comes in different forms: sometimes it's physical, sometimes psychological, sometimes emotional, and sometimes spiritual.

Breann "Bre" Lasley is a Salt Lake City entrepreneur who started a business teaching English as a second language. In the wake of a harrowing assault that left her fighting for her life, she found a new purpose. In 2016, Bre founded an organization called Fight Like Girls, hoping to encourage and empower girls and women. Since then she's spoken to thousands of people, telling her story and inspiring others with her strength and spirit.

When I read about Bre's experience, I thought about the visceral elements of survival and self-preservation that play a part in cultivating hope. I decided to ask her if she'd be willing to talk to me about that — and about anything else she'd like to talk about — and she readily agreed to sit down with me.

The plan is to meet up at the Salt Lake City Public Library this afternoon. But I have a one-year-old, so things seldom go as planned. Chloé squirms in my arms when she hears Mom's voice over the car's Bluetooth phone.

"Mom, can you please watch Chloé while I meet Bre Lasley? Everything has gone over schedule today, and —"

"Elizabeth, I told you to call Bre six months ago," Mom says in her I-told-you-so voice.

"What?"

I vaguely recall Mom's message on my enormous to-do list. A girl had been badly hurt. Mom thought it might help if I talked to her. But until this moment, I hadn't connected that wounded girl to the dynamic woman I'm scheduled to interview today.

Mom says, "I'll watch Chloé as long as you tell Bre that I told you to call her."

"Yes, yes, of course. I'll tell her."

Chloé is always excited to see Mom, and today is no exception. I drop her off with a quick hug and kiss and jump straight back into my car, speeding toward Salt Lake City. I had suggested the library as a meeting place, thinking it would be the perfect spot, filled with quiet people studying or working. A safe place for difficult questions. It's a beautiful building I'd like to explore further. Luckily, a parking spot is available. I'm running late, so this couldn't be more perfect. I pull in, check my recorder, and head toward the library, which is surrounded by a grassy lawn, trees, and . . . homeless people.

My heart turns over.

Please understand: I have great compassion for homeless people, because I *have been* a homeless person. During the time I was being held captive, I walked the proverbial mile in their shoes, sleeping on the hard ground, begging for spare change, eating from garbage cans or going hungry. But I'm worried about Bre. I'm trying to put myself in her shoes now. It's been years for me; for her, it's been just a few months since a homeless man invaded her home and almost killed her.

Imagine, if you can, that you're sitting in your bedroom at night trying to finish a few last emails when you hear a voice say, "Hey!" You disregard it because you live in a duplex and have neighbors who frequently have friends over. You wander into your sister's room to say good night. When you return to your bedroom, a strange man is coming in through your window.

"Hey, girl," he says in a raspy, druggy voice. "I'm coming in."

And he does. He comes in. And he has a knife.

That's what happened to Bre. In the next moment, she was fighting for her life, and in the six minutes that followed, her life was forever altered.

And now I've asked her to meet me at the public library, which is more like homeless central. I'm sorry, but I can't be politically correct right now; I have to be firmly on Bre's side today.

Bre waves when she sees me. She is strikingly pretty, with an engaging smile. I'm surprised to find that she is so petite. How could she have survived such a brutal attack? There's nothing about her that says *victim.* Not a whiff of fear. She has the posture and stride of a woman who has taken her life back. I know immediately that we're going to be friends.

"Are you okay with . . ." I look around uncertainly, but Bre waves off my concern.

"I just thought, *Hey, if Elizabeth Smart can walk through here, so can I.*"

We laugh and start talking like we've known each other for ten years. It feels like we've been chatting for only a few minutes when my phone rings. It's my mom, calling to tell me that Chloé is tired and I should come pick her up. I look at my watch. "Oh, dear. It's been over an hour already, but we haven't even begun talking about the reason I asked to meet in the first place." We both laugh at that. All I can do is beg to reschedule — and not at the public library. Bre graciously agrees to meet at my house, where Chloé will be happy, and we'll be fine, even if we run long.

Nonetheless, a week later, sitting out on my back deck enjoying the warm June sunshine, I'm determined to stick to my list of questions.

"Bre, what was your life like earlier on the day you were attacked?"

"I was excited," she says. "My sister, Kayli, and I had just moved into a new house a week before that — in a safer neighborhood than we had been previously living in. I remember calling my mom two days after we moved in, telling her that I was just so excited and happy about my life. My business was about to take off, and I was super excited about it."

Bre smiles, remembering the kind of details my mother recalls about the day I was taken, small things that loom large and precious when you realize that you were *this close* to losing it all. It makes me think about how oblivious we can be at times — myself included. Life sometimes feels like it's going along smoothly, and suddenly, something sneaks up on you from behind and takes a big bite out of you. How can a person feel safe after that? Bre and I agree: *Home* always meant sanctuary, and the thought of someone invading that sanctuary unbidden was abhorrent. It was easy to push that thought away and think, *That would never happen to me.*

"Kayli had just fallen asleep," says Bre. "I heard a man's voice. *Hey, girl. I'm coming in.* I looked over and there was this bald man — shirtless — coming through my window. And I automatically thought, *He's going to rape me.* So I jumped off my bed and ran towards him to try and push him out the window, but by the time I got to the window, he was already in. He came in headfirst and then was standing back up when I got to him, so we met face-to-face. I remember putting my arms up above my face and saying, 'Please no, please no,' and then he just started hitting me, so I started hitting him back. I got on my knees and started hitting him where you're supposed to hit a man. I'm punching this man in the groin as hard as I can. He's supposed to fall down, curl up into the fetal position, and I can run away. But he didn't even flinch."

She laughs a sharp, unsteady laugh. "Of all the thoughts I could have in that moment, I thought, *Wow, every boy I have ever known is a liar, or is seriously exaggerating how bad it hurts to be hit in the groin.* But then I realized that he was on drugs. He told me to shut up and cooperate. I told him I wasn't going to cooperate. I thought if I could get him out into our dining room, there's a big window, so maybe a neighbor would see us. I tried to pull him out of my room, and he was getting really angry. He shoved his hand over my mouth and pushed me up against my door and said, 'Cooperate with me or I'm going downstairs to get your little sister.' That's when the fight got really ugly."

Bre stops herself, because the story has begun to tumble out of order, the blur of moment-by-moment memory tangled with details she vaguely realized at the time or learned in the aftermath: That this man had been watching them. That he was on crystal meth. That he was twice her size and armed with a knife. Fueled by adrenaline and sheer terror, she thrashed on animal instinct, clawing and kicking the intruder as he dragged her from her room to the kitchen.

"I don't know how to explain it," says Bre. "I guess it kind of felt like slow motion, like it went on forever, and . . ." She shakes her head. "Do you want me to go on with this?"

"If you want to." I leave it up to her. Whenever I speak with anyone, I always want to remain respectful and never push people too far or force them to talk about things they aren't ready to talk about.

But Bre is surprisingly calm as she goes on. "Physically, I couldn't scream — and I was trying to. I remember thinking, *I don't want Kayli to see him. I don't want Kayli to see him.* But then I saw Kayli running up the stairs just swinging her arms, and she was fighting from the very get-go, screaming at him — they were screaming at each other. The man lifted his leg and kicked Kayli down the stairs. Her body didn't hit the stairs once. The only thing that stopped her body was her head going through the wall. Her head literally went into the other room — and this was the only wall in our house that wasn't made of brick. He was so strong. I just thought, *It's done.* But then I realized I still had my phone in my hand. So I shouted, 'Siri! Call 911!' And Siri said back to me — and I'm not joking — 'I'm sorry, Bray. I don't understand.' I was like, you've got to be kidding me! First of all, my name is Breeeee, not Braaaay, and second of all — now is not the time to not understand. Siri should always understand 911."

Bre's bang-on impersonation of Siri gives us both an opportunity to laugh, to take a breath and break the tension. But seriously, I couldn't agree more with Bre: Siri should *always* understand 911.

"Siri did finally come through and call 911," she says. "I saw the little timer start on the screen, so I knew the phone had been answered, but I couldn't hear if anyone was talking or listening. I just kept yelling our address."

This is the kind of incredibly quick thinking that can save a life. Kayli shouted at Siri too. The attacker was confused, pausing for a moment, asking, "Who are you talking to?" But then the battle raged on. From the kitchen, Bre and the intruder tumbled down the stairs to the basement, where Kayli beat him with a metal pipe, and Bre kicked and punched. For a moment he was able to wrench them both into a headlock, rasping, "Damn . . . I didn't think you were going to be this strong." Then Kayli broke free. Bre says a strange calm came over her when she realized that the man had the knife in his hand.

"I said, 'Kayli, he has a knife,' and then again, 'He has a knife.' I was so calm, she stopped screaming. I could tell for the first time she was scared."

Bre told her sister to go for help. Kayli ran up the stairs, out of the house and into the street, leaving Bre in the basement with the attacker, who began stabbing her. He plunged the knife into her stomach and thigh, punching down hard enough to leave deep bruises around the jagged wounds.

Looking at Bre now — petite, slender, a featherweight — it's hard to imagine how she managed to survive. But here she is, telling me what happened calmly, even casually. She's mentioned multiple times already that it was her sister who was the fighter and that she was the one who was scared, but I disagree; she had to be a fighter to survive everything she's telling me.

"It was dark. He fell on his back, and I fell on top of him, my back pressed against his chest. I was only wearing my underwear, and I remember feeling so disgusted that I was with this person in such an intimate position. I felt so violated. He lifted his legs over my legs in some kind of wrestling hold. There was nothing I could do with my lower body. I tried pulling his arm down to try to get the knife away from my neck, but I will never forget the feeling of the cold blade and his flexed hand up against my throat. I thought, *This is really it. There's no way he is going to miss slitting my throat.* I was able to turn my head a fraction of an inch, and I saw black-booted feet descending the stairs."

While Bre struggled with the intruder, Kayli had run down the street, screaming. Officer Ben Hone heard her. He hadn't been dispatched by 911; he was returning home after following up on some other business in the neighborhood. Even with his windows rolled up, the air-conditioning on, a K-9 in the car, and music playing, he could hear Kayli screaming for help. As he got out of his car, Kayli changed her screams from "Help!" to "He's stabbing my sister! He's stabbing my sister!" Officer Hone ran back down the street with her, calling for backup as he charged into the house and down the stairs to the basement.

"I heard him say, 'Salt Lake City Police! Drop the knife!' I never felt so relieved in my life." Bre bites her lip. "Only, my attacker did not drop the knife. The officer repeated, 'Salt Lake City Police! Drop the knife!' Two more times. My attacker still didn't drop the knife. He whispered, 'I'm going to kill you. This is it.' As he extended his arm to slit my neck, his head moved out from behind mine. That's when Officer Hone shot him in the head."

Listening to Bre talk quietly about all the procedural details that followed, I feel the numb horror she and Kayli must have felt as they waited for the ambulance, bleeding and shivering on the porch outside the house where the stranger lay dead. She makes a wry observation now about herself and her little sister, whose pajamas tend to be somewhat racier than Bre's: "The two of us sitting on the front porch looked as different as humanly possible — it was like *Little House on the Prairie* meets *Sex and the City.*"

Again, I'm amazed at how Bre uses a moment of laughter to lighten the intensity of the conversation. We've all listened to and read books about gunfights. We've seen action movies and shoot-'em-up adventures on television. We've certainly seen and heard gunfire reported on the news, but I couldn't imagine the feeling of a bullet whizzing just an inch or two away from my own head, and Bre confirms that it was all a little surreal. The scene seems like something out of a James Bond movie: a fistfight, a metal pipe, a knife, and then finally a bullet to the head. Do we really live in a civilized society when we find that *entertaining*? Or is the primitive human barely concealed under a civilized façade? Do we watch that sort of thing on TV so we can keep it at a distance rather than seriously consider what we would do in a physical "kill or be killed" situation?

Thankfully, most of us will never face that moment. It's terrifying to think about human predators that live and hunt in our world and prey on innocent people who are smaller and physically not as strong as they are. But it's comforting to know that size doesn't matter. No matter how much larger than you your attacker is, statistically, you do have a better chance of survival if you fight back. Bre gives me confidence that small is mighty, and that we can give ourselves literally a "fighting" chance to survive.

Every time I speak, I talk about how each one of us goes through his or her own trials. I try to tell people that it's not what happens to us that makes us who we are, but how we react, the choices we make moving forward. It doesn't matter what our current struggle is; it's what we do about it. But there's a long road between knowing that and putting it into practice. Bre's situation definitely is not normal — it is extreme — yet here she is sitting across from me, happy and moving forward. She's even able to find some humor in everything that has happened to her.

"At first it controlled me," Bre admits. "At first I was playing the victim role, which I deserved to, but it came to a point where I couldn't function. It was controlling every aspect of my life. I'm a very independent person — at least I was before. I've traveled, I've lived abroad by myself, I've done so many things alone, and all that was taken away in one night — in *six minutes,* to be precise. It controlled me until I realized I needed to make a decision to take my life back. Up until that moment, I wasn't sleeping at night. My dad would stay up with me all night, and then I would sleep in the daytime when my parents were around and I felt safe. I didn't want to shower because I would have to close my eyes. And I felt sorry that because of me, someone was shot."

This throws me for a loop. "Wait. *You* felt

sorry for *him*?"

"I felt guilty that he was killed because of me. Obviously, with time . . . well, that's irrational. Of course you're not guilty. But in the moment, I felt like it was 100 percent my fault."

"Was there a moment," I ask, "or was there something that happened that made you realize, 'This wasn't my fault. I don't have to feel this guilt'?"

"Yeah." She nods, knowing exactly the moment I'm talking about. "I had been studying a talk called 'Choose to Believe' by Elder L. Whitney Clayton in the Mormon Church's spring session of General Conference in 2015, and it kind of came back to me, just like — *Whoa, what am I doing?* It woke me up. It wasn't my choice to come in through that window. That wasn't me. And yeah, my attacker's choices affected me, but they don't have to anymore. As soon as I realized that, it's like something clicked, and I haven't felt guilty since then. There was another thing: comparing his choices with my officer's choices. Why am I so focused on his choices and how they're affecting me? Why don't I focus on Officer Hone's choices and how they affected me instead?"

I'd never thought about that sort of focus

as a conscious choice, but I immediately saw the power in her decision.

"What about Kayli?" I ask. "How has this affected her?"

"It affected us differently. It happened Wednesday morning at 12:01. She went back to work on Monday. She doesn't want to talk about it. She's ready to move on, which is great, and I was envious of that, because that was not my reaction. For a long time, I was comparing our reactions and saying there must be something wrong with me, because I couldn't get over it. I needed to make the decision to reclaim my life. As soon as I knew that I was going to live, that my sister was okay, and that my attacker was dead, I thought my fight was over, and then I realized that my fight had only begun. There was a mental fight and emotional fight as well as the physical fight. I already knew the importance of self-defense, but people would tell me, 'You should've clawed his eyes out' or 'You should've punched him in the groin.' "

I cringe at that, having heard a thousand similar comments since I came home. *You should have run faster. You should have screamed louder. You should have kicked him where the sun don't shine.* People say these things, I think, to reassure themselves that they could never be victimized in a similar situation. What happened to you could never happen to them because they would get out of it with some quick-thinking maneuver. This "Choose Your Own Adventure" outcome feeds the fantasy that we can always control what happens to us, and that fantasy is a lot less scary than the old proverb "There but for the grace of God go I."

"I was finally like, you have got to be kidding me," Bre huffs, frustrated. "If people are doing this with me right now, what are they doing with people who are suffering mental illnesses, emotional pain, or eating disorders?"

"So what did you do about it?" I ask.

"I met with my detective, and he told me only 20 percent of women fight back; 80 percent of women are raped and/or murdered because they don't. So I've started Fight Like Girls. My goal is to help raise awareness for other girls to keep fighting. Fight Like Girls will be a place where anyone can get resources to keep fighting whatever it is that they're fighting, and to let people know that self-defense isn't just a physical defense. That you need to be defending yourself in every single way that you can be. It's *self*-defense for a reason, not 'body' defense."

When I was kidnapped, I developed a thin shell around myself, trying to protect myself inside. Whenever Mitchell raped me, whenever he and Barzee hurt me or forced me to do things I didn't want to do, my self-defense was to retreat inside my shell. It was like I just disconnected from reality, and many times that is how I survived. Whether or not you physically fight back, you do what is instinctual, and for me, that was disconnecting and hiding in my shell. I did that while I was kidnapped, and I did that after I was rescued whenever I felt threatened.

One Sunday morning just a few weeks after I was rescued and returned home, my family and I were at church. I had been fighting a cold for a few weeks, and my nose was running like Niagara Falls. I excused myself from the congregation and went to the ladies' bathroom to try to find some relief in blowing my nose. A woman followed me in and stood in front of the door with her foot wedged to the bottom of the door so that no one could come in. She was wearing lots of beads draped around her neck, lots of big rings on her fingers, a long skirt, and bulky shoes. She began by telling me that her father had kidnapped her, and that after she had gotten away from her father, she had met Brian David Mitchell. She said that she knew him, knew that he would never hurt anyone. She started peppering me with ugly questions. "You really loved Brian David Mitchell, didn't you? You really ran away, didn't you?"

I was a young girl who'd just been through nine months of hell. Now, just when I thought I was in a safe place, this weird, scary woman was in my face, slinging these obscene questions, demanding answers. I simply shut down. The only self-defense method I knew was to retreat back inside myself and disconnect. I just stood there, frozen. But my sister came to my rescue. Mom had sent Mary Katherine to look for me when I didn't come back after a few minutes. Mary Katherine, who was a scrappy little eleven-year-old, rammed the door as hard as she could, pushing the woman aside and giving me my chance to escape. When I got back to where the rest of my family was sitting, the meeting was almost over. I sat next to my mother, a hard knot in my stomach as I briefly told her what had happened.

When we got home, Mom told my dad what had happened. Dad took both my sister and me into his office and started lecturing us on how no one had the right to question me or make me feel bad, and I could no longer just freeze up when cornered.

"You need to yell and scream!" he said. "Go ahead. Yell. Try it right now. Scream your heads off."

My sister and I caught each other's eye in a sideways glance, knowing that we were both thinking the same thing: *Dad has lost his marbles.*

But he insisted. "You're not leaving my office until I hear you scream the biggest, loudest scream I've ever heard."

We both giggled. It seemed so silly to be screaming in Dad's office when we were both perfectly safe, but we acquiesced and screamed. Loud. Maybe not as loud as we screamed at our brothers when they entered our room unbidden, but loud enough to satisfy Dad's request. It felt so odd to be doing the very opposite of what we had been taught to do our whole lives. We'd been taught to behave ourselves, use "inside voices," and be quiet, polite, well-mannered girls. It was strange to let go of all that and stand there screaming our heads off.

My parents contacted the police and were told we could press charges. "But chances are, it would just stir the media frenzy," the authorities added. "Do you really want that?"

My parents have always, at all costs, wanted to protect me to the utmost, and this time was no different. They decided that it would be more harmful to press charges and have a court appearance and go through being re-scrutinized by the media and the public. But they did tell other members of our congregation and asked them to let us know if they saw anyone who looked suspicious.

The following Sunday, my parents were traveling back from New York, and my grandparents were in charge of us until their return. The day started off like any other normal Sunday; everyone was in a mad rush, trying to find matching socks and something that wasn't wrinkled to wear to church. I suppose finding something not wrinkled was more difficult than usual because my mom wasn't at home, but other than that, it was a typical Sunday. We all trooped out the door and headed to church. When we arrived, my brother Andrew noticed the same strange woman lingering around the building. He immediately pointed her out to my grandpa, who alerted several other members of the congregation.

I didn't actually witness the foot chase, but I was told that they lit out after her and pursued her through backyards and across streets until she finally disappeared into the Salt Lake City Cemetery. At that point, the police were contacted again. They were able to find her and inform her that if she approached me or my family again, there would be severe consequences.

That's the thing about screaming out loud — or at least telling people what's going on — instead of being stiff-lipped and trying to tough it out alone. People who love you want to know if you're in pain or in trouble. They want to come to your rescue in big and small ways. The people who love you are part of the muscle and teeth with which you fight back.

I'm so happy that Bre is speaking out about self-defense being more than purely physical defense. It is so much more: mental, emotional, and spiritual.

Mary Louise Zeller is a sixth-level black belt tae kwon do master, twenty-time U.S. national gold medalist, and nine-time world champion whose tutelage has produced over a hundred international champions. I'm not sure what I was expecting to learn from Mary Louise when I reached out and asked her if I could interview her for this book, but nothing about Mary Louise is what one would expect.

I knock on the large front door of her house in South Jordan, a pretty, quiet community outside Salt Lake City. The door opens, and here is this woman in her early seventies with short brown hair and bright red lipstick. She has one leg bent, resting on the kind of medical scooter they give you after an orthopedic injury or operation. The weather outside is overwhelmingly hot, but she looks cool and immaculate.

Mary Louise jokes, "I just had surgery on my foot. A thousand kicks a day can make a world champion but apparently takes a big toll on my foot."

Walking into her home, I notice the care and attention to detail that seem to abound in every aspect of her life. Matthew and I had recently remodeled our kitchen and had had to compromise on our countertops, so I immediately notice that she has the exact rough-hewn edge on her granite that I had wanted. Her dining table is beautifully laid out, with the proper salad plates, forks, and goblets. She invites me to sit down and tells me, "Everything we're about to eat is organic, natural, and homemade." Hearing this, I'm not sure what I'm more excited for

— the food or the conversation. As it turns out, both are amazing.

"I wasn't always like this," Mary Louise tells me over lunch. "I was raised in Atlanta, Georgia, where girls don't fight."

She briefly describes the somewhat ordinary life she lived until one fateful day when she was forty-six years old. Mary Louise and her family were visiting friends who had recently moved into a new home in California. The house had large windows running floor to ceiling. The happy group of friends were upstairs on the second level, admiring the magnificent view and chatting while Adam, Mary Louise's eighteen-month-old son, played nearby. In the space of just a few seconds, Adam ran to the windows to look out, pushing himself against the screen to get the full effect. The screen tore away from the window, and baby Adam fell headfirst to the ground two stories below. People outside saw the whole thing and said that Adam landed on his hands and knees and bounced as he hit the ground. Mary Louise rushed him to the hospital and spent the next several hours in the ER, numb and shaken to her core, gripping the tiny hand of her critically injured son.

Though I already know that Adam did eventually make a full recovery, I still shudder at the thought of his little body hurtling toward the ground. My beautiful little Chloé is eighteen months old right now, and I feel like I have to have one eye on her at all times. She's constantly trying to make a break for the horse pasture across the street or opening the cabinets under the sink where all the cleaners and detergents are. Yes, of course, I have childproofed multiple times. And of course, Matthew and I always try to watch her, but stories of a toddler slipping away or getting into something or falling from something are surprising only if you've never had a toddler in your life. It takes less than a moment, so there isn't a moment in the day that I'm not thinking or worrying about Chloé.

When Matthew and I first brought her home from the hospital as a newborn, I felt like my heart had been dislodged and relocated in my throat. I no longer could do anything without feeling this new sensation of love, anxiety, protectiveness, and complete adoration. We were discharged from the hospital with a perfect baby, but a day later, her pediatrician said she was jaundiced. Being a brand-new parent, overbearing and overprotective, I about had a nervous breakdown. I was crying my eyes out, refusing to set Chloé down. It's my worst nightmare that something could happen to her, and that includes worrying about myself being an overprotective mother. I think it's fairly understandable that I might have some deep-seated feelings about the vulnerability of children.

This firestorm of conflicting emotions rings familiar to Mary Louise. In the wake of her son's accident, she tells me, she struggled. "I had post-traumatic stress disorder. The counselor told me I needed to spend a couple hours a day away from the baby, because I was hypervigilant and hyperprotective. I saw an ad for tae kwon do that said it would improve mental clarity, improve focus, and improve fitness — all the things that I needed at the time — along with developing self-confidence after I had been literally shattered."

"I've never tried a form of martial arts," I tell her. "You're so passionate about it, I'm really starting to wonder if I've been missing something in life."

"No other sport did for me what tae kwon do did," she says. "The sense that I could stand strong in the face of all the bad stuff, and I could empower others to be stronger. I think for women especially, we get attacked because we're the 'weaker sex.' Skill is really good. I tell people, 'I'm a very old woman of seventy-two, but I know things you don't. I can do things to you. It wouldn't go well for you.' It's a bit of a joke, but it's a little true." With a mischievous sparkle in her eye, she adds, "Actually a whole lot true. I would hope if someone attacked me, they'd wake up in the hospital wondering, *What happened? Wasn't I the one attacking* her?"

Mary Louise leans forward, looking at me so intently I feel like she is trying to see beyond my face, right into my very being.

"We all leave this earth," she says. "We all die, and we don't get to know what comes next. It takes a lot of courage just to live life. If you're feeling like you're powerless, like life is bigger than you, like bad things can happen and you have no power to stop them, there's something about the martial arts rather than yoga, or aerobics, or weight lifting, that leaves you with a sense of power."

This one sentence, more than anything else Mary Louise has said, rings true to me: *It takes a lot of courage just to live life.*

While I was kidnapped, my captors moved me to California for the winter. We initially lived in an old riverbed that was actually a lot like the fire swamp in the movie *The Princess Bride*. We stayed there for a couple

81

months before my captors decided that it was too close to people. They started searching for a new hidden camp. They eventually found it: an isolated place far up a mountainside so steep we had to crawl on our hands and knees to reach it. After the move had been made, I was no longer allowed to go out in public. I was held captive at the hidden camp night and day. Barzee was my constant jailer when Mitchell went for food and supplies.

One day in February, Mitchell and Barzee got into a huge argument. Arguments were in no way rare; they happened frequently. This one was like a raging inferno. Both Mitchell and Barzee were whaling on each other. Usually Mitchell would say in his sickliest, sincerest, calmest voice, "Hepzibah, Hepzibah." (That's what he called her.) "I love thee. The Lord hast heard thy cries and wants to speak with thee. I need to give thee a blessing." Then he would give her a "blessing" and tell her how special she was, how she was on the right hand of God, and how she had a throne and a crown awaiting her in Heaven, if she could only endure this life and the weaknesses and shortcomings of the Lord's servant and prophet, Immanuel. All this was done to calm Barzee down so he could keep on doing what he was doing and make Barzee not only deal with it but accept it as needful. (I'm honestly getting a little sick just writing about it.) That was how he would always get his way with her.

But during this terrible fight, he didn't fall back on his usual line. Instead, he grabbed his little money pouch and stormed out of the hidden camp, yelling over his shoulder, "I'm going to minister." (By that he meant he was going into town to beg and steal.)

I said hardly anything that day. We'd had very little to eat the previous few days, and despite being hungry, I didn't want to incur the wrath of Barzee or tempt her to vent her frustration on me. I remember going to bed very hungry that night. The following day was even harder, if that was possible; we had no food or water. I was starving. We did eventually catch some rainwater. I remember drinking as much as I could, but then I had to go to the bathroom. I was so light-headed when I stood that by the time I made it outside and over to the bucket that we used as a toilet, I almost collapsed on the rough rim. I made it back to the small tarp shelter, crumpled to the ground, and didn't move the rest of the day.

A week went by before Mitchell returned.

At this point, all thoughts of hope and escape had disappeared, and I was trying to make peace with myself and God before I starved to death. Maybe that was childish — thinking I would die after only a week of not eating — but I was just so hungry, I didn't think I could go on much longer. All of a sudden, in the midst of my silent prayers, I heard a voice singing. Not a pleasant, angelic voice. It was a voice I recognized and hated. There was Mitchell, singing a hymn as he tramped back into the hidden camp as if he were a conquering hero. I don't recall which hymn — he ruined so many good ones — but it could have been "I Need Thee Every Hour." Or maybe "There Is a Balm in Gilead." He started talking about all that had happened. As it turned out, he had been in jail, and because it was Christmas weekend, the three-business-days holding period turned into seven days. He talked about the bed he'd slept in, the food he'd eaten, the hot showers he'd taken, and the relaxing time he'd spent in jail.

Oh, how I envied that lovely jail cell! Unbelievable. I was practically dying of starvation and thirst. The condition in which I was imprisoned made a stint in county lockup sound like a luxurious vacation.

Then he had the audacity to pull out the leftover remains of KFC, as if he were providing us with a Christmas Day feast. Truth be told, it might as well have been a Christmas Day feast. The stale chicken was greasy and tough as leather, and my stomach felt shrunken and fragile. I couldn't eat very much, but I told myself I couldn't stop. I had to force myself to choke down as much as I could. I couldn't forget my resolve to do whatever I had to do to survive. I had to eat whatever I could get my hands on. I had to drink dirty water. I could not allow myself to lie down and die.

It takes a lot of courage just to live life.

I think of Mary Louise running down the stairs, calling her son's name, knowing that he might be dead when she reached him. But hoping . . .

"What is hope?" I ask her now, and she settles her chin in her hand, thinking about it for a moment.

"What I've learned," she says, "is that hope is first created in language. We hope for better things in life, and life has not-so-good things too. Then who do we *be* after something bad happens to us? It occurs here, in our mouth." She touches her finger to her lips. "What do we say about it? What do we create? We literally create with our language. 'I'm going to be a champion' or 'I'm going to be a world-class international marketer.' But hope for me is empty in language if there's not action to realize it. In language, you create possibility. You create the hope. You create a new possible future, and then you take action — to learn from those who have more experience than you and to do the work. Even in the very beginning, I was practicing two hours a day. I'm happier when I'm fully engaged in a project that makes a difference. That's when I'm happy. That's when I'm most alive. That's when I'm most well. I think human beings thrive on that."

I take all this in, tracing the handle of my spoon with my finger, pondering my next question, but before I can ask it, Mary Louise sits back in her chair and asks me, "What have you found? Did you get better when you started talking and wanting to make a difference for others?"

The short answer would be yes, but I don't get the sense that Mary Louise is the kind of person who goes for the short answer.

"Initially," I tell her, "when I first got home and everyone was saying I needed to see a therapist and doctors and I needed to be debriefed and hospitalized and all these things, I remember thinking, *There's nothing wrong with me. I don't need to talk to anyone. I'm fine. Just let me be. I needed help when I was with my captors. I don't need help now.* I think I felt that way for a long time, and I think time did a lot of healing for me. I wasn't able to go back and reclaim my old life, but I was able to go on to high school and continue on to college. I did study abroad in London. I did my mission in Paris. I think that time was very healing for me — just continuing to experience life."

"Bad stuff happens," Mary Louise says quietly. "I was date-raped — and back then, I felt stupid. Guilty. Responsible. I wasn't! But that takes its toll on you. The thing is, I don't have to *become* that. I can't ever forget it, but I don't have to doubt or mistrust myself. What is hope but creating better life in the face of all the misery?"

I notice the afternoon sun stretching across the dining room floor. I've stayed longer than I intended, and if it were up to me, I'd stay another hour, but I decide to limit myself to one last question. "Mary Louise, do you believe in happily ever after?"

She nods a sharp, sure nod and declares, "I do. Along with all of it — all the imperfection — I think we can create as much perfection as we can. Like in the physical environment I try to create in my home. Cleanliness. I don't do it myself now that I can pay for it, but I have done it myself. I'll clean this place to the nth degree, like Jesus is coming over for dinner, and I'll create something beautiful to my eyes. I think that creation of beauty, trying to create the best of life, that gentle part of life amidst all the imperfection . . ."

She digresses a bit, talking about *Downton Abbey* and her cats, but eventually she finds her way back to the original question.

"I do believe in living happily ever after. I already am," she says. "I believe in fairy tales. But you have to be willing to do the work to make them come true. Sometimes you have big goals, and you don't reach them, but you accomplish great things in the process. It's worth all of it. I didn't know what I was doing with tae kwon do; I just kept doing it because I was most alive when I was doing it. I didn't like the feeling of just taking care of my home and my family. They're precious to me, and I like that, but it's not all there is to me. I don't know what else I'll do in my life, but I'm going to live it fully. I have had some grand experiences."

So this seemed to be another vote for happily ever after — if you're willing to fight for it. That fight may happen as it did for Bre in a violent, six-minute blur that had no greater goal than physical survival. Or that fight may be the long fight that happens in the heart. The fight to reclaim calm and happiness after our strongest doors have been broken down, our safest havens invaded.

"Even then," says Mary Louise. "That's just a choice. *Let's go live great.* I've got a great opportunity — let's go live a great life."

It seems to me that the choice she's talking about is another form of self-preservation. In the past ten years, I've come to understand that self-preservation extends to self-care. You can't ignore your personal needs in any situation. Yes, there are situations where it is impossible to attend to all your personal needs, but at the very least, you have to give yourself credit for being human and needing whatever it is that's missing. If you have no food, you have to at least acknowledge your hunger. You can't just pretend it doesn't exist. When you have a chance to stop and listen to yourself, you have to take a moment to redigest, decompress, and recognize your feelings and emotions about what's been going on.

Take a moment to be alone, or talk to a friend. Sometimes taking care of yourself means doing something you love, indulging a passion or engaging in a hobby. Sometimes it means finding a therapist or a therapy to suit your situation. Whatever your unfulfilled need is, it's dangerous to swallow or ignore it.

Most of the time, the courage to live happens on a much smaller scale than it does in dramatic or traumatic moments. I survived a major traumatic event when I was a girl, but I'm still beaten down hard when I'm pregnant and exhausted and my baby girl is running a fever and throwing up all night. Everyday struggles take their toll, and I think most of us — especially working moms who've been trained to put ourselves at the bottom of every to-do list — sometimes need a reminder to just check in with ourselves:

What do I need from this life?

What's truly at stake here?

And what am I doing to fight for it?

3
SEEING A RUSH OF RED

Bitterness is like cancer. It eats upon the host. But anger is like fire. It burns it all clean.

— MAYA ANGELOU

Anger is perceived as a negative emotion, but in fact, it plays an important role in the healing process. Anger is a natural sensation, a sign that you're human, that you're past feeling sorry for yourself — and that can have a positive effect, as long as you don't get mired in it.

Growing up in America, most of us are taught to answer the question "How are you?" with "Fine" or "Good." When I lived in France for a year and a half, I was always surprised when I asked someone, *"Comment allez-vous?"* and they actually told me! They'd delve into their private lives, worries, and woes. It taught me to appreciate genuine honesty when asking the question

"How are you?" It also taught me to respect the question, because we shouldn't be asking it unless we are genuine in our interest or concern. We shouldn't ask the question if the person being asked is not allowed to answer honestly, but there are things we're trained to mask, and for women in most world cultures, expressing anger is a big social taboo.

Norma Bastidas, who was born in Mexico, is a professional athlete and an advocate for victims of human trafficking. I first met her when I was pregnant with Chloé and working on a video raising awareness, hoping to help people better understand that not all prisons are made of iron bars. When I ask her, "So, Norma, how have you been?" I'll admit, initially, I'm just being polite. But I like the honesty with which she answers.

"You know, it's actually not been . . ." Norma sighs deeply and gets real. She immediately has my attention. "Probably you're the only person that I can tell the truth. I'm terrible, terrible, terrible."

I'm surprised by Norma's candor, but I appreciate it. Her honest anger is refreshingly authentic. I settle into a side chair in my living room and set my phone on speaker, knowing that the best thing I can do right now is listen. I'll ask questions later.

"Another big article came out about my story," says Norma, "and that's always — I pretend I'm okay, but it's very, very difficult every time a story comes out."

Norma's father died very early in her childhood. The extended family stepped in to help as much as they could while Norma's mother took on additional hours at work to support her children. Norma's maternal grandfather started to pay extra attention to her, grooming her for the day he raped her when she was only eleven years old. It was a horrible situation for this little girl. Her mother was working all the time to feed and clothe her children and keep a roof over their head. Meanwhile, Norma's maternal grandfather and someone else close to the family were sexually abusing her.

To me, as firmly grounded in family as I am, this is an unthinkable betrayal. Your family is supposed to love and protect you, but this child found neither love nor protection. She finally saw a way to escape the abuse and sexual violation when a talent agency offered her a modeling job in Japan. Norma was young — only nineteen — and at first, it seemed an answer to prayer. Unfortunately, it soon became a living hell. In the beginning, she was given an apartment and money to send back to her family. She felt good about helping her mother and siblings, but soon the "modeling agency" started asking her to go to nightclubs and dance. They firmly reminded her that she needed to work off her debt — the airplane ticket, the apartment, the money she sent back to her family — and soon, dancing wasn't enough. They wanted her to allow certain gentlemen to pay her for very specific services. And it was done in a cleverly coercive way. Of course, they insisted, they were just "suggesting," not forcing or demanding. It always looked like Norma was free to do as she pleased. Two bodyguards stood outside the bedroom door, but the "agency" insisted that this was for Norma's own protection, so that "clients" couldn't get rough with her. All that was as far from the truth as possible.

This shadowy organization had brought her into a foreign country illegally. She didn't speak the language and had no money, no friends, no family. She had no recourse if things didn't work out. She felt isolated and alone. When Norma finally escaped what many people would probably call "prostitution" but what is more accurately called "human trafficking," she returned to her family in Mexico. But everything was different. Word of what had been going on in Japan had made it all the way back to her hometown. One day, she was kidnapped and raped multiple times. You would think that the community would have rallied around her with love and support, that outrage and horror would have been directed toward the monsters who had hurt this young woman so badly. Instead, she found herself isolated again by a wall of shame and ignorance.

Neighbors who had known Norma her whole life turned their backs on her. She eventually relocated to Vancouver, British Columbia, got married, and had two kids. It seemed that she had left her past behind her, but the pain did not go away. In time, it broke her marriage, and amid the stress of becoming a newly single parent of two children — one with a degenerative eye disease — she lost her job. All the problems of the present struggle combined with the weight of a horrific past that could understandably destroy anyone.

Desperate to find some kind of relief, Norma started running — and she didn't stop. She ran until she found she could run a whole mile. Then she ran until she could run ten. She ran until the pounding of her feet slowed down the constant pounding of her heart, until the constant beat of judgment, shame, violence, and loneliness sank into the rhythm of her own steady pace. Within six months of putting on her first pair of running shoes, Norma qualified for the Boston Marathon. She didn't stop there. She became an ultramarathoner, running races of 50 miles and more. She has since competed on all seven continents. In March 2016, she took on the challenge of a triathlon. She swam 122 miles, biked 2,132 miles, and ran 735 miles, and she didn't just beat the world record, she obliterated it.

Norma was strong before she ever started running or being a triathlete. She was born strong. She survived more than most of us will ever be faced with. Some of it has left her deeply, justifiably angry. And she's strong enough to acknowledge how she truly feels.

"I understand that every single time I accept a request to talk about my path in a media story, it's going to be difficult," she says. "I take steps not to revictimize myself, but it's hard to completely avoid it. Every single time I open a chapter, there's always backlash. Family members were upset, just because nobody wants to be attached to that negativity. It's hurtful when family members are like, 'Could you please just not talk about it?' It's hurtful. It's hurtful because it *happened* to me. Everybody just wants you to pretend like it didn't happen, but that doesn't help victims or future generations in which a change could be made."

Listening to Norma speak, I feel a kinship with her. I have a pretty good idea how she must feel right now. Our experiences are different, but there are a lot of similarities — similarities that can be found in all types of exploitative experiences, from kidnapping and human trafficking to domestic violence and bullying. There is one word in particular that I and probably most survivors of anything find especially intolerable: *Why?* Not "why" in the sense of our asking ourselves, "Why did this happen to me?" but in the context of others asking us, "Why didn't you run, scream, say something, go for help, fight back, et cetera." Most people don't think they're asking anything rude or being insensitive, but these questions are damaging, because when you ask, "Why didn't you . . . ," the victim hears, "You should have . . . ," which translates to "It's your own fault that this terrible thing happened to you." Intentional or not, that is how it often sounds. And there are two points I'd like to make here.

First, we are not God. We do not have the power to decide whether or not this person deserves what happened to them. And second, we don't have the right to ask those questions. Survivors don't have to share anything they don't want to, and we need to respect their privacy. To be asked to relive this horribly painful part of our lives and then to be questioned on whether we could have or should have done more than we did to help ourselves is, frankly put, insulting. The truth of the matter is, this person being questioned survived. So that in and of itself is a big deal. The fact that they are standing there speaks to validate what they *did* do. Sadly, some situations cannot be survived, no matter what choices are made in the moment. In any case, I can promise you, this person did all they could, fighting harder and holding on longer than any of us can imagine.

I survived. Bre Lasley survived. Norma survived. Each of us did what she had to do. What matters is that we're here to tell about it, when and if we choose to. Not only did Norma survive, she broke barriers to make a small mark on history, and she repeatedly puts her privacy and vulnerability on the line in an effort to change the way victims of human trafficking are perceived and treated. I feel strong empathy for the aggravation she feels when she's misquoted or trotted out as a cautionary tale.

"That is so frustrating, Norma. I'm so sorry."

Simply being heard and understood allows her to release some of the tension from her voice.

"It's okay," she says. "Why open up the story if it's not to educate or change, right? There's a reason why we're all here. I'm not saying they should give us a medal. But it's time to get everybody to understand why this microaggression is not okay."

Microaggression. That's not a term I hear very often, but I know exactly what it means, and chances are you do too. Common examples of microaggression include giving backhanded "compliments" like "You're really pretty for a fat girl." Or telling a gay man, "You just haven't met the right person yet." It's a slap in the face dressed up as small talk, a "nice" way of saying something hurtful.

The most infuriating example I can cite from my own life occurred when I was twenty-one years old. I had recently broken up with a long-term boyfriend and had decided to serve a Mormon mission for my church. While I was filling out paperwork and making all my doctor and dentist appointments, a friend talked me into a blind date with a guy she thought was really nice. I was focused on my mission trip, not looking to start any kind of relationship, but I was assured that this was just casual, just for fun. The date itself was all right, nothing special or exciting. The guy enjoyed talking and did a lot of it. I'm pretty good at listening, so that's basically how the evening went, which was fine. But on the way home, he started talking about my kidnapping and the abuse that had happened. Just as we arrived at my parents' house, he said, "You were raped so many times. Was there any moment that you were just like, 'Okay, I'm being raped,' and enjoyed it?"

Of all the interrogations, interviews, question-and-answer sessions, and court proceedings I've been through, to this day, I have never been asked a question equal to that in stupidity, insensitivity, and complete and utter ugliness.

Date. Over.

Footnote: This moron came up to me in public not long after this, fell to his knees weeping, apologized, and — brace yourself — asked, "Will you marry me?" I can't even imagine what he expected me to say. *Yes?* And then he'd carry me off into the sunset? I don't think so. The only words that came to my mind were, "I'm going on a mission."

I was on an airplane to France the next day, and I've never seen that guy again, thankfully, but the Mormon Church is a small world. I heard through the grapevine that he showed up at a meeting attended by a friend of mine, and by way of introducing himself, he got up and said, "My name is [forever synonymous with 'idiot'], and I almost married Elizabeth Smart."

I'm still baffled. Some people.

This is a vivid demonstration of microaggression and the cluelessness that usually accompanies it. It's more often about stupidity than malicious intent, but that doesn't make it cut any less deeply. It still hurts and revictimizes.

"When the CNN article came out," Norma says, "people started to offer support to my husband, calling him 'brave' for dating someone or for marrying someone like me. It's actually incredibly hurtful. Why does he deserve a medal for marrying me? It didn't affect him, and it had nothing to do with him. It's not like that. If he had been a victim of a carjacking, people wouldn't come to me and say, 'You're amazing! Your husband was carjacked, but you decided to go ahead and marry him anyway.' "

I cringe at that familiar refrain. "I'm

dumbfounded when people say that same sort of thing to Matthew. Even if it is meant well, it's still just shocking to me. Norma, what do you do when you feel the way you do today?"

"There's a comfort zone, I'm understanding. The wall comes up, and I just shut down to all of their crap. I just walk away from a lot of social media. Once I start feeling uncomfortable, I simply tell everybody I need some time off. I only allow people in my life that make me feel comfortable."

Definitely, there are times when I need to be alone, to recenter myself and get back to who I truly am. There are times when I want to speak out about something other than this one thing that seems to define me in the minds of a lot of people. And there are times when there are people who think they can push me further than I am willing to go.

One experience pops straight to the front of the line in my memory. When I was sixteen, my dad and I went to Washington, D.C., to promote the bill for a sex offender registry that would require all sex offenders to report where they live, when they move, what state they're in, et cetera. The idea was to create a blanket effect so that offenders wouldn't be able to get lost in the cracks and abuse more children. I'd had a long day, speaking to different legislators and doing the media circuit. We did so many interviews, I don't even remember whom else we spoke to, but Dad was proud of how his young daughter was able to stand up and articulate the need for this law, to put a face on it and bring attention to it. This was important work, and I was grateful for the opportunity to do it, but I was relieved when my dad said, "This is the last one — a lady named Nancy Grace."

Call me sheltered, but I had never heard of her. Dad explained that she was a very big deal and had a highly rated show on HLN. Going in, knowing that this was the last interview made me happy. I sat down on the set. She wasn't there in person; the interview was going to be conducted over satellite. My father and I were given our earpieces, and microphones were clipped to our collars. Before the show started, a female voice with a southern lilt came on, introducing herself as Nancy Grace. She said she wouldn't be asking me anything I didn't want to talk about. We briefly talked about the sex offender registry being the reason my father and I were there in D.C. — and on her show — and my dad made it clear that we weren't there to talk about anything else.

The show began, and her southern lilt took on a breathy edge.

"Elizabeth, I remember when you first went missing, and literally hundreds of people were out looking for you. Now we know you were being held captive not very far away from your home *at all.* Did you ever hear people calling out your name, trying to find you?"

It caught me off guard, but I knew immediately where this was going. I sucked in a deep breath and felt my protective shell clamp shut. She leaned in, waiting for me to answer.

"There was one time," I said. There was an expectant pause, but I didn't want to feed the beast that was lurking just under the surface of this conversation. I'd heard these questions a thousand times: *Why didn't you scream louder? Why didn't you run faster? Why didn't you kick him in the groin, because that always works, right?*

"At that moment," said Nancy, "did you want to scream out, 'Here I am'? 'Help me'?"

I kind of wanted to scream when she said that, actually, but still trying to be a team player, I said, "I mean, of course. Who wouldn't?"

She belabored the insinuations — the microaggressions — mining for gory details. I gave terse, tight-lipped answers until she gave up and said in a patronizing tone I'd heard many times in the year or so since I got home, "It's hard to expect a little fourteen-year-old girl to react the way an adult might imagine they would react under those circumstances. You were *afraid,* I assume."

"Yeah." *No shucks, Sherlock.* I rolled my eyes a little and glanced at my dad, who was starting to look like he would soon have steam coming out of his ears.

She forged ahead. "Did your kidnappers tell you they would hurt you or your family if you tried to get away?"

"You know, they did. And I really am here to support the bill and not to go into what happened to me, because I'm not here to give an interview on that. I'm here to help push this bill through."

"And I *want* you to push the bill through," she said earnestly. "And I *want* people to hear — your — voice."

This rang a little hollow, as people were mainly hearing her voice not talking about the bill. The way she said it let me know in no uncertain terms what was expected of me here. Mug shots of Mitchell and Barzee were already being projected over my face as the interview continued to go downhill.

"You know, a lot of people have seen shots of you wearing a burka." Nancy shook her head and smiled as if she was asking me about a Halloween costume. "How did you see out of that thing?"

At that point, I had had enough. I'd gotten past the initial jolt and was gathering a nice glow of bright red anger. "I'm really not going to talk about this at this time," I told her flat out. "I mean, that's something I just don't even look back at, and to be frankly honest, I really don't appreciate you bringing all this up."

She quickly offered a classic sorry-not-sorry apology, as smooth as honey butter, emphatically forgiving me for disappointing her. "I'm sorry, dear. I thought that you would speak out to other victims, but you know what? I completely understand."

Just a side note: Don't ever say you completely understand what someone else has been through in their life. You don't.

"A lot of victims don't want to talk about it," Nancy went on, "and don't *feel* like talking about it. Let's talk about the bill. To Senator Hatch. Senator Hatch, you said you wanted . . ."

Abruptly, Dad and I were shut out. Our

mics and earpieces were turned off, so we could only see what was being shown on the screen. My dad was about to burst. He got up and said, "Come on, Elizabeth. This is ridiculous. We're leaving."

Members of the camera crew all ran up, whispering, "The segment isn't finished. Sit down, sit down. You can't leave yet!"

"Watch me," Dad said.

But by that time, the segment was on the wrap-up. We said a terse *Thanks for having us*, and it was over. Needless to say, that was the first, last, and only time I ever went on Nancy Grace's show. I have certainly grown and learned a lot in the twelve years since then, but even as a teenager, I knew that you have to do what you think is right, and you have to stick to your guns. The fact is, I did speak out for other victims. I did speak up about what happened to me. I still do. But I'm not obligated to share my story on cue just because someone else wants me to — just as Norma is not obligated to keep her story to herself. Each of us owns the story of herself; it's a personal choice when and where to share it. Others have the personal choice to listen or not, but they have no right to push us into the limelight or back into the closet.

"I stood my ground this time," says

Norma. "I said, 'This is my right, and if you are uncomfortable, you're welcome to step back and not be part of this process. You don't have to come. Don't read articles; don't come to any of my talks. You have that right. Absolutely. But do not stand here and make me responsible. I refuse to apologize for anything.' "

I'm so proud of Norma for standing her ground. I understand firsthand how difficult it can be to stand up for yourself, whether it's against someone you know or someone you don't know. I was a pretty shy kid, and that really didn't change after I got home. In fact, there are days when I need to disconnect and just be another onlooker in the crowd. But there are times as well when I have to overcome my shyness and take my own stand. It's important to set boundaries and stand your ground and know that no one has the right to push you further than you want to go, whether it's someone you love — like a spouse or a family member — or anybody else.

Questions will be asked that are insensitive and ignorant. I hear this from people in so many different situations — cancer, divorce, sexual assault, the loss of a child — and I tell them that it's perfectly acceptable to be angry, and I mean both angry about what happened and angry about the gall of some people's responses to it. The important thing is that you address your anger, acknowledge it, feel it, and then move on.

It took about eight years after my rescue for my case to finally come to trial. I've been asked if that was frustrating, and yes, in some regards it was terribly frustrating, but I also look back and wonder, *If it had happened immediately, would I have been ready for it?* I hadn't wanted to talk about the kidnapping at all when I got home. I remember thinking, after I'd gone through all the necessary questioning by the FBI and other branches of law enforcement, that I never wanted to speak about it ever again. And so for those eight years, I was able to go to high school and then on to university. I studied abroad, and then started serving my mission in France. In a way I had been given a reprieve, a chance to discover who I, Elizabeth Smart, really was. So in that sense, maybe the delay wasn't such a bad thing.

But the trial had to happen eventually, and I knew that getting through it wasn't going to be easy. I was called back from France to testify. The first day of the trial, part of me was quite nervous, because I hadn't been in the presence of Brian David Mitchell in eight years. I didn't know how I would feel seeing him in person again. Thankfully, I had a lot of family by my side.

I have to digress here for a minute and tell you about Grandma Smart, who is full of zest and vitality and has a flair for the dramatic. She knew that it was going to be hard to find a parking spot near the courthouse, so instead of driving herself there or calling a car service or a taxi, she walked outside her house, waved down the next car to pass her, and said, "I'm Elizabeth Smart's grandmother. Could you drop me off at the courthouse, please?" And that is how she arrived there — she hitchhiked. This tells you everything you need to know about Grandma Smart.

The court proceedings were long and grueling. I spent three days on the stand. I wasn't allowed to hear my mom or sister testify; I had to sit outside. The rest of the time, I sat in the courtroom and listened to testimony that made me wonder, *Who thought it was a good idea to have that person testify?* I'd been warned that Mitchell's attorney would go to great lengths to mount a strong defense. Some testimonies were almost comical, they were so non sequitur, but others were outrageously ugly and hurtful. I lost my cool only once: during testimony by Dr. Paul Whitehead, who had been assigned to observe and work with Mitchell in the Utah State Hospital. Dr. Whitehead, who had spent what was, in my opinion, a pitifully small amount of time observing Mitchell, went on about how I had been looking forward to becoming pregnant with Mitchell's child and how I had even chosen a name for the child.

At that moment, all I saw was a rush of red. In the middle of his testimony, I completely lost my composure, stood up, and marched out of that courtroom as fast as I could. I was absolutely fuming. I'm surprised smoke wasn't coming out of my ears. I don't remember ever being that angry.

What Dr. Whitehead didn't say was that my captors (always planning ahead) had forced me to keep a journal. I was told exactly what to write in it. That's where this "expert witness" had gotten most of his information. That journal was something I had hoped would never see the light of day. I was embarrassed and ashamed that my hand had ever written anything like that, but the truth is, I did what I had to do to survive. That journal was their ultimate weapon against me, something they could use to deny the harm they'd done me and possibly go free to harm someone else. From the moment I got home, I wanted it burned. I never wanted anyone to see it. Maybe it doesn't seem like much in the context of everything these people did to me, but to this day, that is still an object I never want to see again. I hope it is incinerated.

I suppose the judge must have been taken aback when I abruptly stormed out of the room; up until that point, I had remained calm, emotionless, composed. He must have paused the proceedings, because next thing I knew, my parents were searching the building for me. I had gone to a different floor. I just wanted to be alone. Once I realized what I had done and how it might have looked, I also knew that I didn't want to be questioned about why I was so angry or upset. I just wanted to be left alone. I remember thinking, *How would Dr. Whitehead like it if his life were being publicized and put under a magnifying glass, and people who spent next to zero time doing what they should have done — who knew and understood nothing about what it was like to be Mitchell's captive — were testifying as an "expert" for the opposing side?* In contrast, the prosecution had spent hundreds, if not thousands, of hours on research, observation, and interviews.

After the brief break, I did regain my composure, and the court was recalled to order so the proceedings could continue. That court experience was neither easy nor enjoyable. It had interrupted my life — and my mission — and brought back my most difficult and painful memories. But that trial did one thing for me: It confirmed that neither Mitchell nor Barzee would ever have any power or control over me ever again. Mitchell's attorney tried to have him sent to a mental hospital, but he was sentenced to life in federal prison without parole. Barzee pled guilty and was sentenced to fifteen years. But more important, I walked out of there knowing that I had survived, that I was in fact thriving. Their lives were effectively over, but mine had just begun, and I would never have to think or speak of them again except on my own terms.

Toward the end of my conversation with Norma, I ask, "So many people have hurt you. Do you feel like you've forgiven them?"

"That's a difficult one," she admits. "I think the biggest thing was forgiving myself for something that I felt I had done wrong — that I blamed myself for — because I did believe it. Forgiving myself was a really big,

big step. Really looking at myself and saying, 'I still didn't deserve it.' For so long, I did that. Why didn't I scream? Why — all those whys. And now I don't. I just forgave myself. I did not deserve any of it."

"What about forgiving others?"

"Forgiving the other people is harder for me. The people who did those things had no excuses. None were ever compelled to come clean. Not even one of them went to prison. I don't really know about forgiveness. Having said all that, I have been applying to work as a sexual aggression corrections officer. I've been working with victims for so long, and I think that that's how I would learn a lot about forgiveness: by switching gears and applying for a job that's going to make me responsible for the people who are the criminals in the system. Only because I understand that I need to be better. I cannot have this hatred. I think it is a value of being better than the people who caused the pain. Showing kindness to the people who probably don't deserve it — that's one of the most difficult things. I still have a hard time feeling sympathy for somebody who, in my case, doesn't deserve sympathy, just because they've done something and now they're caught and stuck in the system. That's kind of something that

I'm working on, but it's not going to be an easy thing for me, for sure."

I'm equally sure it's not easy for anyone else, but I agree with the Buddhist proverb "You will not be punished *for* your anger; you will be punished *by* your anger." I believe that we have to be honest with our anger and work to tame it so that it energizes us instead of incinerating us. So I admire Norma's startling desire to help sex offenders survive in the prison system — her way of powering past this blaze of anger. It can't be smothered; it has to burn itself out.

"I want to grow as a person," she says resolutely, "and I think the more I understand both sides, the better able I am to help. Because I'm able to offer one point of view, but I've made a commitment: If I do this, it better be with the intention of really helping as much as I can. Being a beginner and putting yourself in a position of others teaching you is what gives you humility instead of standing onstage, saying, 'I know it all.' I don't! I'm still managing, sharing a little bit. It is an intention of being able to learn more and more, and being able to understand it from both sides, how they are, and handle it."

Putting it that way, she confirms the very feeling that prompted me to go out into the world and ask these questions I'm asking. When people ask me about anger, I know they're talking about Mitchell and Barzee, but the fact is, during the trial, I realized that I had let go of that anger a long time ago. Right before the court proceedings began, Mitchell appeared, marched in by guards, shackled, and arrayed in a prison jumpsuit. I listened to my heart for a reaction, but amazingly enough, there was nothing.

I wasn't intimidated. I wasn't infuriated. I felt nothing.

Not nothing in the sense that I was numb. I had strong feelings about life in general. That day, like today, I keenly felt all the gratitude and joy and love that I feel every day of this beautiful life I have with my family. People say living well is the best revenge. But why would I want my life to be an act of revenge? Doesn't that just extend a tormentor's occupation of your head?

Which isn't to say I never get angry. Every now and then — especially when I hear another story of a child who's been abducted or a woman who's been grievously harmed — I feel that rush of red. There's no bitterness, but there's anger — "righteous wrath," Scripture calls it — clean and proud and powerful, and sometimes it gives me the strength I need to stand up for what I know is right.

My conversation with Norma left me thinking hard. Could I even imagine giving up my current occupation to work in prisons with sex offenders, child molesters, and kidnappers? I honestly don't know. Truly, I would have never thought of that as an option — a way to learn, to overcome anger, to forgive — and I'm not sure it is an option for me. Is it for you?

Can you see yourself stepping into the perspective of someone who's wronged you and using that new understanding in some positive way?

And if not, can you see your anger energizing some other positive direction?

4
LOSS AND RENEWAL

Grief is in two parts. The first is loss. The
second is the remaking of life.
— ANNE ROIPHE

Grief is one of the emotions people don't
know how to help with when they're looking from the outside in. We often feel
uncomfortable around people who are
grieving — and it's okay to feel that way.
Totally understandable. But it helps to
recognize that there is a beauty and a
strength of character that emerges as we
grieve. Washington Irving wrote: "There is a
sacredness in tears. They are not a mark of
weakness, but of power. They speak more
eloquently than ten thousand tongues. They
are the messengers of overwhelming grief,
of deep contrition, and of unspeakable love."
Virtually everyone growing up in Utah
recognizes certain names that we almost
think of as dynasty families, and one of

those names is Covey. That name rings a bell far beyond Utah, of course; Stephen Covey wrote the best-selling self-help book *The 7 Habits of Highly Effective People.* The Covey family is well established in the Utah community, involved in philanthropy, community service, and nonprofits. I don't remember the first time I heard of the Covey family, but I do remember my first interaction with them.

In 2015, I received an email from a nonprofit group called Bridle Up Hope, which was founded by the Covey family in memory of Stephen Covey's granddaughter Rachel, who had died in 2012 at the age of twenty-one. They asked me if I'd be willing to speak at a gala they were holding to help raise funds to build a private stable for the sole purpose of helping young women. They explained how they worked in equine therapy, how they focused on working with girls who experienced depression, anxiety, and other mental illnesses, and that to date, they had never turned away one single girl. I didn't know anything else about the story behind Bridle Up Hope. I wondered but didn't feel free to ask how Rachel had died so young. I was intrigued by their mission and eager to help, however, partly because instead of asking me to dive back into the gory details of my past, which is usually what people want to hear, they wanted me to speak about my experiences with horses and how they had helped me.

Horses and riding with my grandpa definitely made an enormous difference for me after I was rescued. When I came home, my parents allowed me to make as many choices as they could. Among those choices was whether or not to seek therapy. Offers for therapy were coming out of the woodwork, but I remember thinking, *Where were you when I was kidnapped? That's when I needed you.* I chose not to go down the traditional therapy road but instead found therapy through music, through my parents and family, through taking back my life. I also found it through horseback riding in nature, experiencing that wide-open feeling that I had when I was out riding with Grandpa Smart. He never pushed me to talk about anything. He just stayed close enough that I could feel safe without feeling confined. He would occasionally look over at me with a twinkle in his eye and then that was it, we were off galloping as fast as the wind until the horse and I were both drenched in sweat and my nose was sunburned to a crisp and my limbs felt like ramen noodles. Freedom, more than anything, was what I needed. I had to breathe that freedom under the bright blue Utah sky I loved. I had to feel upright and strong again, which is how I felt riding high up in my favorite saddle.

The night of the Bridle Up Hope event, I was thinking, *Okay, this is a horse-friendly group. I should wear my cowboy boots!* Unfortunately, they were a little too dirty and a little too scuffed-up to pull off with a floor-length black skirt. What's a girl to do when she doesn't have the right shoes? Turn to the old standby black stiletto that goes with everything, but maintain that cowboy boot attitude.

When I arrived at the event, there were already dozens of people there mingling and chatting, among them my parents, who had also been invited. As the night progressed, my nerves progressed too. Usually, I don't get nervous; I'm not worried about what I'm going to say. But somehow, that night it was different. Any time my parents are in a crowd where I can see them, I almost always shed a few tears. It's not sadness; it's more an acknowledgment of the pain they went through and a moment of realizing that their love for me extends beyond realms I ever thought possible. And that night was no exception.

After my talk, I didn't want to seem rude

or cold, but I really just wanted to be by myself to allow myself to feel what I was feeling without having to explain it to anybody. Plus I always feel a little awkward when I cry onstage in front of people. So I was hoping to slip away as quickly as I could, but then Rebecca Covey stepped to the podium, her chestnut hair and classic evening dress impeccably but gracefully styled. She spoke briefly in a warm, welcoming voice about her daughter Rachel. All I knew about Rachel was that she had passed away; I didn't know how. I saw the portraits of Rachel, a beautiful girl with a broad smile and a strong chin: Rachel sitting with a fluffy little white dog in her lap. Rachel focusing intently with her hands poised over the strings of a harp. Rachel on horseback, flying like the wind. I listened to Rebecca speak of her with that same unconditional and abiding love that my parents have for me. The sound of her voice and the radiance of Rachel's smile stayed with me for a long time. As I made the list of people I wanted to interview for this book, I thought of Rebecca Covey and sent her an email that I hoped was not too forward. It had been over a year since we'd last seen each other, but she said she'd be happy to help in any way she could and invited me to her house so we could sit down together for a quiet conversation.

It's boiling hot outside as I pull up in front of Rebecca's house. All morning, Chloé has been vocal about how she thinks we should spend the day, and none of her ideas include her car seat. She practically explodes from the seat as soon as I have the buckle undone. Walking up to Rebecca's home, I notice the beautiful yard and think briefly about how nice it would be to spend the day playing among the flower beds and bushes with Chloé instead of struggling to restrain her in my arms while trying to conduct a very serious conversation for the next hour. Knocking on the door, I feel a little bit anxious. Almost intimidated.

The door opens, and two of Rebecca's children — a nine-year-old girl and an eleven-year-old boy — smile up at me. I smile back at them and say, "Hi, I'm Elizabeth. Is Rebecca home?"

They run off to find their mother. She appears and invites me in. Rebecca looks the same as she did the night of the gala over a year ago. She has her long dark hair swept into a ponytail, and when she smiles, there is no questioning the kind of mother she is: patient, generous, kind, and calm. Inside the house, it's cool and quiet and full of memories. I notice Rachel's beautiful gold harp behind French doors. Pictures of family hang on the walls and stand on shelves. Even though I feel anxious and a little nervous, there's a familiar feeling. This isn't just a house; this is a home that has known both joy and sorrow.

In the movie *The Devil Wears Prada,* Nigel (played by Stanley Tucci) says fashion is "greater than art, because you live your life in it." As I see it, a home is greater than any other structure, because we live our lives in it. A truly beautiful home — like the one I'm standing in now — is vibrant with life. It's not just a show house or a museum where everything has a place and nothing is to be touched. It's lovely but lived in, and people who come knocking at the door feel more at ease because of it.

Rebecca leads me into her husband's office, and we sink into a comfortable sofa. I set my little digital recorder between us and begin with the question I always start with: "Would you please introduce yourself briefly? Just for the record."

"I'm a mother," says Rebecca. A simple statement, but there's great pride, purpose, and meaning in the way she says it. "I love being a mom and helping my kids with their lives, helping them in the right direction. I also run a nonprofit foundation called Bridle Up Hope: The Rachel Covey Foundation, in honor of our daughter Rachel, who passed away in 2012. That's who I am and what I am focusing on right now in life."

I study Rachel's portrait on the wall. She looks like the quintessential girl next door, her intelligent blue eyes full of fun. She has the polished look of someone who took time to get ready for a portrait but who would probably prefer to have her hair in a simple ponytail and be racing outside to go for a horseback ride, looking for the next great adventure.

"What was Rachel like?" I ask. "Some families have the peacemakers, or the family clowns. How did she fit into the family?"

"Rachel was the second mother," Rebecca says. "Wyatt, my youngest, would call her Mom too, because she was seventeen when he was born. She was very nurturing, really fun with the kids. If the kids had a project for the science fair, it was Rachel saying, 'You should do this.' Then she would help them build some amazing thing. She was very creative, very hands-on, and had a good relationship with every one of the kids. I think that was kind of her role. That's why it was so hard for us to lose her, because it was like she was so close to everyone and such an integral part of everyone's lives."

"The Bridle Up Hope website mentions that Rachel had a great love for animals. When did you realize that she loved them so much?"

"I would say it started when she was tiny — eighteen months old," says Rebecca. "I didn't grow up with animals, and I didn't really like animals, so we didn't have any, but my in-laws had a dog, and Rachel just adored that dog named Sheldon. She loved that dog so much that we got her a rabbit, and then a cat, and one animal led to another, until then it was a horse. She loved them all. In fact, once she saved her money and bought a chinchilla. I was really picky about where the animals would have to be, like in the garage. I was a bit of a germ freak. I feel really bad about it now." That thought makes her catch her breath for half a second, but then she smiles, remembering the chinchilla story. "I didn't know anything about it for months until my three-year-old said she was scared to go into Rachel's room, and when I asked her why, she said, 'Because there's this little animal in there with these whiskers.' Anyway, I had to laugh, because it was just like Rachel."

I have to laugh, too, at the idea of this bright, softhearted teenager hiding a furry friend in her room.

"She was just drawn to animals," says Rebecca. "Loved them. She was a really sensitive soul, a really sweet, sensitive soul."

It's not hard to imagine Rachel, the way her mother talks about her. I can feel that sweetness in the way the family interacts. Looking at the portraits of the pretty young girl smiling down at me, I see ample evidence that she was anything but ordinary. It's easy to visualize her walking through the family's kitchen and stooping to pick up the cat, only to put her down again, turn around, and play the harp that now stands silent behind the glass panes of the French doors. She seems like such a bright spirit, a girl to whom the laws of gravity barely apply. What could have happened that ended her life so soon?

In preparation for this conversation, I had read everything I could find about Rachel and the foundation. There was not much about her personally, but the foundation's website mentioned that Rachel suffered from depression. I would have preferred to dwell on horses and chinchillas, but I need to understand the rest of the story, and Rebecca knows this is why I've come.

"Did Rachel suffer from depression her whole life," I ask, "or was there a time you noticed a change in her?"

"I would say it probably started about seventh grade, when she had a hard time focusing at school. That's where it started. When she was younger, she had a lazy eye — one eye would cross — so she wore glasses. She struggled in school. She didn't like to read. She had a hard time focusing. I took her to a doctor, and he put her on some medicine for ADD, and it was really bad. We took her off, and she seemed to resume her normal self, fun and loving. Then it seemed to start again in high school, maybe her senior year, when she started getting depressed."

From the corner of my eye, I see that Chloé has completely ransacked my diaper bag and purse and spilled peanut butter M&Ms all over the floor. "Oh, shoot. I'm sorry." I apologize and try to wedge Chloé between my knees. Having recently taken my own dogs to the vet after they ingested a variety of forbidden treats — ibuprofen, grapes, chocolate — I worry that one of the Coveys' multiple pets will get into the M&Ms, so I quickly kneel to clean them up.

"Don't worry about it," Rebecca says. "I'll just close the door and clean it up later. I've got a whole basket of toys. Would Chloé like to play with them?"

There is no doubt that Rebecca is a mother and has been in the same situation, trying to entertain a toddler while trying to accomplish something much more serious at the same time. I gratefully accept the toys for Chloé, and while Rebecca gets her interested in them, I pick up the rest of the candy. Rebecca smiles at Chloé, perhaps remembering happier days when her children were still little.

"Rachel's senior year in high school," she says, "that's when I started noticing the depression and anxiety. I had never been around it, so it wasn't . . . I didn't understand it. I just thought she was being lazy or that she didn't like school, so it turned into a negative thing. The negative feelings towards school and homework often trigger negative emotions in the parent like, 'Come on, you've got to get your assignments in.' She was just so right-brained, just so creative. She played harp — did all the Suzuki harp camps — was an amazing harpist. She was an artist. She would sew. She was very crafty."

Listening to Rebecca, I'm a little stunned to realize how similar Rachel and I were while we were growing up. We were both the oldest girls in our families, both loved animals, especially horses, both played the harp and attended Suzuki harp camp. I'm surprised I never knew her.

Rebecca says, "I decided not to focus so much on school, and why she wasn't getting her homework done, but just focus on the positive. That was kind of a transition for me as a mother, realizing that not every child is the same and that you're going to have some kids that are book smart and do really well on tests, and you're going to have some kids that like to be outside with horses and have an amazing creative side to them."

After Rachel graduated from high school, she went to Brigham Young University — another thing we have in common — though she went to the Idaho campus, where she came to a startling realization, Rebecca tells me. "She calls me and says, 'Mom, I think I'm dyslexic. I think I have dyslexia.' She came home that weekend, and we took her to a learning specialist who tested her for dyslexia — and she had dyslexia! I never knew that. She went all the way through all of her school years, and I never knew it. I just thought she didn't like to read. We felt so bad. But for her, she said, 'That makes sense now. Now I can totally see why school was so hard for me.' "

Rachel was also diagnosed with auditory

processing disorder, a sort of disconnection between what the ear hears and what the brain comprehends, which has been linked to ear infections, head trauma, and premature birth.

"When she would read a paragraph, she would put different words at the end and then at the front so by the end, she wouldn't understand what she just read," says Rebecca. "She ended up coming back to Utah and enrolling in a vet tech program at Broadview University. When you study dyslexia and depression, they kind of go hand in hand. Many people who have dyslexia have depression as well, and I think it just got worse and worse. But because I had never had gone through depression — I didn't grow up with it in my home — I didn't know. I feel like I was a naïve mother who didn't realize the seriousness of it. Now that I'm looking back, I'm just like, *Why didn't I recognize that?* She *did* struggle with the anxiety. The depression got really bad to where she wouldn't even go to school to do her vet tech program. Then we took her to a doctor, and he put her on an antidepressant. That's what I feel really hurt her the most, because a lot of times people are on antidepressants, and it's good and it helps them, but then there are those other people that . . . it doesn't help them . . . and doctors don't know how that person's brain is going to react to that antidepressant."

Rebecca straightens her spine. Her jaw takes on a certain set.

"I don't want to get into all the negative of it," she says, "but basically, parents need to be more aware, and they need to educate themselves and figure out that there are alternatives to antidepressants. One is exercise. One is being in nature, yoga, other types of things that can do so much good."

This rings so true for me. I do believe in the power of modern medicine and medication, but I also believe that there are many other healing options. I can speak firsthand to that. After I was rescued, I had so many people suggesting therapies, therapists, hospitals, treatment centers, places I should go and stay to be debriefed and then reintroduced to society. And I have no doubt that most of those different methods have merit for some, but for me, they wouldn't have been right. I needed to be at home with my parents, who listened without pushing me to talk more than I wanted to and offered wise counsel without pretending to truly understand what I'd been through. I needed the freedom to sort through my own thoughts and make my own choices. Horses and nature were extremely healing for me, and I also found peace through playing the harp. I agree with Rebecca that the answer is to help educate people that there is more than one right way, that all options should be considered. You keep trying until you find what works for you.

"After Rachel had been on medication for some time," Rebecca says, "it just wasn't working, and she called me and said, 'I don't feel myself. I feel like someone else is in my head, like there's someone else in my brain or something. I'm not myself.' We knew that. She said, 'I'm going to come off them.' You have to wean yourself off them, but I don't think she did. I think she just went cold turkey. I think what happens is . . . your mind just does crazy things. We personally feel that . . ."

Again I see the resolve, the self-determination in Rebecca's shoulders, but now I see the tremendous weight she carries as well.

"I just don't like the word *suicide,*" she says. "You know what? It's the reality of it, but we really honestly feel like it was not Rachel. It was not *Rachel.*"

I understand that there's a firestorm of emotional response to suicide in a family, in a community, and in our culture, but I don't get the feeling that Rebecca is shying away from the truth of what happened. And I'm glad I didn't pry into the cause of Rachel's death before I understood the big picture of her life. I think I get the distinction Rebecca is making: the difference between who someone truly *is* at their core and who they are when they feel that core has been usurped or is missing somehow — or even, in a sense, has been kidnapped.

There was a time when I was being held captive when things had grown so dark and painful, the effort to try to keep living so overwhelming, I started to consider what would happen next if I did kill myself. I don't know if I would have done it — if I was capable of doing it. But I do know that I was in a very dark place. My captors had moved us to Southern California, and I was confined to a dirty riverbed where there were rodents and bugs. Mitchell had just tried to kidnap another young girl. For weeks he had been searching for his "next wife," and finally he thought he had found the one. He hadn't actually seen her in real life, but he had seen a picture of her.

He had found some clothes discarded at an abandoned homeless camp in the same dry riverbed about a mile away from where

I was hidden. He put them on, put his beard into a ponytail on his chin, and pulled his hair back into a low ponytail at the nape of his neck. Then he started scouting out different churches. He always targeted the Mormon churches. One Sunday, he showed up at a Mormon church in El Cajon, where he was greeted and invited in to attend the meetings. Later, when Mitchell got back to the camp, he scoffed at the kindness the members and missionaries had shown him, saying, "Ha! They thought they were going to teach me? The Lord's servant? They will all be humbled one day when I am revealed as the Lord's righteous right hand."

Because kindness and compassion are always stressed in our faith, he had been invited to dinner by a family in the church. They drove him in their car to their home. He gorged himself on the Sunday dinner this generous woman prepared and later told me — as I sat there practically starving — every detail of every bite. Almond chicken, steamed green beans, mashed potatoes, salad, fruit. He said, "Deep down, she knew who she was dealing with — the Lord's servant and her future son in-law."

It honestly makes me taste throw up in my mouth a little bit, just thinking about him and the things he used to say. While he was at this family's house, he saw a picture of a young girl on the piano. He asked who she was. The lady said it was her daughter from her first marriage and that she lived with her father but came to them every other weekend and Wednesdays. That was all it took for him to decide that this young girl would be his next victim.

On the night of the would-be abduction, he dressed in the same black sweats he had worn when he kidnapped me. As he very carefully packed his bag, he pulled out a knife. It was the same one he had held to my throat. He asked, "Do you know what this is?"

What an idiot. Of course I knew what that was — as if I would forget something like that.

Then he asked me, "Do you remember what I said to you the night I came and rescued you?"

Once again, yes. Did he really think I would forget the most horrific words ever said to me? And don't even get me started on him "rescuing" me. There are many things that I will never understand, and don't want to understand, but how he could say that he was "rescuing" me and imagine that I believed that — *ugh.* I will forever be dumbstruck and disgusted by it.

He left with the intention of getting that child, and for the next six hours, all I could do was worry and pray. What was I going to do if he came back with another girl? I hadn't done anything to stop him. Did that mean I was complicit in this kidnapping? Was it partially my fault? Was there some part of me that wanted him to succeed so that I wouldn't be alone? So that I wouldn't always be the one their anger was taken out on? Did I secretly long for a friend to confide in and imagine we might find a way to escape together? I suppose deep down I did. I knew it was wrong, and had he succeeded in abducting that girl, it would have haunted me forever, even if it hadn't been my hand that had kidnapped her, or my plan, or my desire. The fact that I had done nothing to stop him weighed on me so heavily that I welcomed it as a miracle that night when he did not succeed.

He came back into camp huffing and puffing like he had just run a marathon. He sat down and immediately began to consume what little food we had. He told us how he had taken the bus to the girl's house and searched around the whole property before he found a sliding door left unlocked. As he started pulling the door back, he heard something, stopped, and listened. When he didn't hear anything again, he continued pulling the door back and started to enter the home. He heard the noise again. I know most people consider snoring a health risk or an annoyance, but in the case of this young girl, it saved her life. When Mitchell realized that what he was hearing was a manly snore, he knew that he would not succeed in "rescuing" — which is to say kidnapping and raping — this girl. After he finished the food and the story of his misadventure, he told us in his most "spiritual" voice that it had been merely a test, like when Abraham was commanded to kill Isaac. The Lord just needed to know he was willing, and the next wife would come, all in due time.

After this episode, I lost all hope that I would ever be found, that I would ever be happy again, that I would ever feel safe again. I knew it would be easier to give up and end it all. I knew that I would be in Heaven for eternity, that I would be with God, free from suffering, reunited with my family. The problem was the act of actually killing myself. I just wanted to die — to magically walk through a door and suddenly be in Heaven, away from this horrible nightmare I was living — but I couldn't imagine how that might be done with the available resources. By what method would this happen? And the more I thought about the particulars, the more I knew I couldn't do it. I realized that if I wanted to live — and I did want to live — I had to find my hope again and cling to it. I couldn't give up.

But I did come very close to giving up. Close enough that I have great compassion and empathy for anyone who feels they can no longer bear to live. So when Rebecca tells me what Rachel said — "I don't feel myself. I feel like someone else is in my head. I am not myself." — I believe her. I always want to be respectful and not intrude, but I feel like I've learned so much about Rachel, like she's a friend. I've never met her, to my knowledge or memory, but there are so many similarities between us. I want to know what happened.

"How did Rachel die?" I ask.

"She was on an antidepressant. She knew it wasn't working and she had adverse effects from it. She couldn't even open her jaw. She had a dentist appointment that I kept rescheduling and rescheduling. She had lockjaw. She wasn't herself. She was in her apartment — and you have to understand, Rachel's never done anything wrong. Ever. She's like a really good girl. Never.

She'd never done anything wrong. She just was really a wonderful, wonderful person. That's why it's so shocking to us. Her roommate found her. She had a four-poster bed. The posts had these really pretty sheer white drapes. Four drapes that came down. She had wrapped the drape around her neck. She wasn't hanging. She was leaned to the side like this . . ."

Rebecca shows me. Leaning a little. Like a swan in a ballet.

"She had choked herself. It's so hard . . . because I could feel something was wrong. And I kept calling her for a couple hours. She wouldn't answer. I told my husband, Sean, 'Could you just run down to Rachel's apartment and see if she's doing okay?' Because sometimes she'd go to the horses and wouldn't answer if she was on a trail ride or something. She had just moved into this cute apartment. My husband pulled up and all the police cars were there and the ambulance and everything. He never got to see her. They wouldn't let him go in. He called me and said, 'Come down to Rachel's apartment. Hurry. There's something wrong.' That's when I went down."

"Nobody had told you or your husband that Rachel had died?"

"Not until I got there to her apartment. I

pull up, and there are cars everywhere. Then the policeman — no, it was the paramedic — he stopped me and said, 'Your daughter's passed away.' It was really, really bad. Just totally shocking to our family. It's hard as a mother, too, because I knew she was struggling, but I thought she was getting better . . ."

I sit quietly with no idea what to say. The profound sadness of the situation is like a dense fog you try to see through but can't.

"This close friend of ours," says Rebecca, "she can feel angels, and she said that she felt Rachel. After Rachel passed away, she felt that Rachel had come to her and had said, 'Can you go tell my parents? I don't know what happened and I'm really, really sorry.' We almost feel like she just wasn't herself. It wasn't her real self. Not long after Rachel died, we met with Elder Jeffrey Holland. He has long been good friends with the Covey family and was so sad for us. He told us that depression is a disease. He said, 'It's like cancer, and it's a sickness, and the sickness took your daughter.' "

I don't for a moment struggle with the notion of angels, but it's hard to pin down the idea of that other self — a wounded self inside the armor of day-to-day life — and I wonder how many people I know are wag-

141

ing that same fierce battle beneath a seemingly calm exterior. I wonder how often we look at a person's smiling exterior and completely miss what is going on inside.

Rebecca and her family are the kind of people who, when bad times hit, don't crumble and fall but rather cling to one another and become a fortress and a safe haven for each other. Rachel's death obviously shook them to their very core, but it seems to me that the more lasting impression on them was made by her life. Something about the bright spirit of this girl sustained them and made them want to go on, to love each other, to get up in the morning.

"What helped you deal with your grief after Rachel died?"

"Two days after," says Rebecca, "we were absolutely devastated, and one of her friends — someone we hadn't seen in years — came to see us, and she said, 'Do you know that Rachel changed my life?' I'm like, 'What? What do you mean?' She said, 'I hadn't seen her since junior high, because I went this direction, which was a bad direction, and Rachel went this direction, which was a good direction.' "

Rebecca sets her hands wide apart, showing what the girl showed her. The girl went on to tell Rebecca that Rachel had reconnected with her and said, "I'm going to teach you how to ride a horse."

"She had been taking this girl on trail rides," says Rebecca. "We didn't even know it. Rachel was helping her. She said it totally turned her life around."

So right then, just a few days after Rachel's death, Rebecca decided to start Bridle Up Hope. (The name was suggested by a friend who breeds Arabians.) It didn't take long for Rebecca to see the impact.

"We've just been moving forward ever since," she says. "We've put about three hundred girls through our program so far. I think it's been really good for our family to have Bridle Up Hope. I think it saved me, because there were points I didn't want to live. When you lose a child — for a mother, it's devastating. You've been with them from the second you were pregnant. The twenty-one years we had with her were so wonderful. It was so . . . so devastating to me. Because you're just like, *What if? What if I had done this?* Then I just realized, I couldn't do the what-ifs. You can't look back into the past. You literally just have to move forward. You can't do the what-ifs."

I'm familiar with the what-ifs. I know what a dark, pointless path they lead to.

"Have you ever felt anger or guilt about Rachel's passing?" I ask.

"Yes," she says. "I've had every emotion. Every single emotion. I think the biggest thing that's helped me is . . . well, a few things. One is, you have to pray for strength to not have the crazy thoughts, to not have those weird emotions, the guilt, the anger, the sadness, the grief. *Why didn't I do this? If only I would've done this.* But it just gets your mind in a frenzy, and you start thinking all these negative things. I learned I had to just stop it. The scripture says, 'Be still and know that I am' — and to me, that means be *still* in your mind. Still those crazy thoughts. When you start thinking, *Why didn't I go over that day? Why didn't I go over that moment? Why didn't I know I needed to go help her that day?* — it just doesn't do any good, so I literally just have to still my mind, and just focus on what's the most important, and just know that she's in good hands, and that she's in a good place, and that she's happy, and that she's helping others. I feel like she's helping on the other side." Rebecca looks intently at me and very honestly says, "Yes. I have found peace, but I am not totally healed yet from Rachel passing away."

She speculates that it may be years before

144

that happens — if it ever does — and in the meantime, she's determined to harness that pain and turn it toward something good. Rachel's story is heartbreaking, but because of her — not because of her death, but because of the girl she truly was during her brief life — Bridle Up Hope has helped hundreds of other girls find their way back to a place of hope. Rebecca Covey found a modicum of peace and an outlet for her grief, working to save the lives of other young women who struggle in the same ways Rachel did. This world would be practically perfect if we all followed that example every time we were struck down by grief and loss in our lives.

Sadness. Grief. Depression. These are three very different things, though they may seem the same on the surface sometimes. Depression is an illness. Sadness is a mood. And grief — it's complicated. Grief can be unclear and confusing, and no two people experience it in the same way. We've all heard of the different stages of grief — denial, anger, bargaining, depression, and acceptance — which makes it sound so cut-and-dried. Like you just move from one box on the flowchart to the next. Three, four, five — done! You're good. I think grief can take you in loops like a roller coaster, so that you visit any of those stages more than once, and I think it's possible to experience more than one of those stages at the same time.

Long before I met Matthew, when he was only eighteen years old, his father, Stewart, died suddenly. Matthew is the second of five children. His youngest sibling, his only brother, was eight years old. Stewart had gone to the doctor to find out why his back was hurting so much. For weeks he hadn't been able to stand up straight. He'd been to see the doctor several times before and was always told to go see a chiropractor or a massage therapist, which he did, but that didn't help. This time was different; the doctors knew something was seriously wrong. After a series of tests and scans, the results came back: Cancer had spread throughout his body, metastasizing to the extent that they couldn't even guess where it had originated. He was told he was terminally ill, but no one could have guessed how swiftly the end would come. He was diagnosed on a Monday; he died that Thursday.

But before Stewart died, he found a moment to speak with each of his children. Matthew told me that when he saw his father, it was hard to even recognize him because his face and body were severely swollen due to the steroids and medication he was on. Matthew knew at that moment that the only way his father would ever come home again was in a coffin.

Stewart died shortly after speaking with Matthew. It was after Stewart died and while his body lay in his hospital bed that Matthew spent a few moments alone with him and allowed his grief to overcome him. He knew his father was dead, and he accepted it, but that didn't make it any easier. He was just a kid. He wanted his dad, not just for himself but for his mum, for his sisters, and for his eight-year-old brother. Matthew has told me that he felt every stage of grief in that moment, a tornado of shock and sadness and loss and fear for the future and gratitude for the past. And love.

In Europe it is not uncommon for the deceased person to return to their home and basically lie in state for a day or two before being buried. When I first heard that, I was a bit uncomfortable with the idea. No one I knew had done anything like that. In the United States, whether a person dies in a hospital or at home, they're immediately taken to a mortuary, where they are prepared for burial. They're brought back out for the funeral and then taken to the grave site. That's what we're used to, and that's what we're comfortable with. But after listening to Matthew's experience, I changed my mind. There's a certain beauty in the European way.

After Stewart died, he was brought home in his coffin so people could come pay their last respects. While he was at his home for the last time, each of the children had the chance to sit alone with him. Matthew has said he knew then that not only had he accepted what had happened but also that no matter how hard it was, he had to keep going.

Isn't it strange and kind of impractical that the moment we lose someone is the moment when we feel our love for them most intensely? We all deal with grief in life. That's just the way things are. The only way you'll never grieve is if you never love anyone — including yourself — so we're left with only one way forward: to embrace grief. It is healthy to grieve when we lose family, friends, loved ones — or when we lose a little chunk of ourselves. We will only destroy ourselves from the inside out if we bottle it up and never let it out. Over and over again, I see that the healthiest way to let it out is to help someone else.

Are you ready to open that door and see a bigger picture beyond your own pain?

Can you imagine yourself feeling less fragile in the moment you turn your pain toward a greater cause?

5
THE SACREDNESS OF FAITH

For we walk by faith, not by sight.
— 2 CORINTHIANS 5:7

My faith has served me through my darkest times. It's been a constant in my life, and it's precisely because I feel so strongly about my own faith that I honor and respect the faith of others. I get a lot of questions about my faith — not about the particulars of being Mormon, but about how I kept my faith and how it's affected my life in general. When I signed up to serve a mission for my church, I had no idea the effect it would have on my life. I knew that I wanted to share with others this faith that had helped me through so much darkness — and that still helps me today.

Sister Smart,
    You are hereby called to serve as a missionary of the Church of Jesus Christ of

Latter-Day Saints. You are assigned to labor in the France Paris Mission. It is anticipated that you will serve a period of 18 months. You should report to the Provo Missionary Training Center, where you will prepare to preach the gospel in the French language.

It was a hot, sunny summer day when I received my mission calling. I was twenty-two years old and had just returned from a semester abroad in England. All my family was gathered around, everyone guessing where I was going to go. Although I had marked in my application that I would like to serve a foreign mission, that is a guarantee of nothing. I could be called to just about anywhere in the world, from Tokyo, Japan, to Austin, Texas, from Wellington, New Zealand, to Fairbanks, Alaska. It was already a huge step for me to decide to serve a mission, and the wait for the mission assignment had felt like an eternity.

When I ripped open the envelope and tore out the letter, I was so nervous I didn't even see where I was being assigned. Then, realizing I needed to read it word for word, I went back over it and let it sink in: I was going to the France Paris Mission. I would be speaking French. Wow. I could hardly believe it. I immediately conjured up an image of strolling through the streets of Paris with a Book of Mormon in one hand and a *mille-feuille* in the other, speaking the most romantic language on earth. I have to laugh now at how wrong I was. I did eat a lot of French pastry — about forty extra pounds' worth — and I don't regret a single éclair, but other than that and the scenery itself, there was nothing romantic about my time in Paris.

Every mission is split up into "areas" that you're assigned to work in. You are also assigned a companion who goes everywhere with you. Women are assigned a female companion, called a "Sister," and men are assigned a male companion, called an "Elder." The only time you're ever alone is when you're in the bathroom. Your time as a missionary is split up into "transfers": six-week intervals during which the area president can, if he feels the need to, change your companion or your area. The first area I was assigned to serve in was a suburb of Paris called Évry.

My first transfer ended up being the most difficult one of my entire mission. I had arrived in France in February. It was dark and cold. The missionaries who were assigned to work in the mission offices dropped off my trainer companion and me late at night after a series of long flights. I was so tired, I fell asleep in the car on the way to Évry and started snoring and probably drooling with my mouth open. My companion shook me and said, "We are here, sister. Wake up." I stumbled out of the car and struggled inside with my luggage, which contained everything I would wear for the next eighteen months: as many skirts, blouses, and panty hose as I could fit into two suitcases. Overwhelmed by jet lag, I just collapsed on one of the beds when we walked into the tiny apartment.

When I woke up the following morning, I stared at the small living quarters around me. The whole apartment could have fit into my bedroom at home. It was a long and narrow studio with a set of bunk beds, two desks, a small galley kitchen, and an even smaller bathroom, but it was clean and seemed safe enough. Cozy, even. The apartment didn't do much to prepare me for the shock I received when I walked around our area. The majority of people were from Africa (Sierra Leone, Cameroon, Côte d'Ivoire, Congo) or the Middle East (Iran, Pakistan, Afghanistan). With my bright blond hair and blue eyes, I stuck out like a sore thumb. People always stared at us, partly because I was so white, I think, and partly because of the name tags we wore on our jackets introducing us as missionaries. It was not uncommon for people to mistake us for nuns.

This mission was such an eye-opening experience for me. I always knew I had lived a privileged life, but I was amazed as I came to understand just how sheltered I really was. We walked into apartment buildings that were condemned, but people were still living there because they had nowhere else to go. The smells were completely overpowering. On the days that I knew we were going to some of these buildings, I used to spray extra perfume on my clothes in the morning to try and drown out the smell. That never worked.

My companion was from Mexico and didn't speak much English. I was fine being forced to speak French because I was trying to learn the language as fast as I could, but I had a feeling she didn't much like Americans. She harrumphed that I was being prissy when I didn't want to walk down dark alleyways or take the shortcut back to our apartment through the dark park at night. Maybe I was being prissy in her eyes, but in my mind, my caution was simply a matter of self-preservation. Sometimes, when I was feeling really sorry for myself, when all our appointments had either fallen through or we had been stood up, I would think, *What did I sign myself up for? Why did I agree to take this kind of rudeness?* Then I would have to remind myself, *Elizabeth, you survived nine months of being kidnapped. You can survive this mission. Stop being such a baby.*

We were always encouraged to talk to people everywhere we went, so during my first week in Évry, as my companion and I were sitting on a bus, I tried in my very remedial French to strike up a conversation with the young man sitting across from me. I asked him if he was from France. *"Êtes-vous français?"*

He politely answered. My French was slow, and his was thickly accented, so I had no clue what he was saying, but then we exchanged some other pleasantries, some of which I actually did understand. He asked me about the badge I wore on my jacket. I told him I was a missionary for my church from America. *"Je suis une missionnaire de l'Amérique. Êtes-vous . . .* um, are you religious? *Religieux?"*

He said something that sounded like, "Moos-li-ma."

In my pathetic understanding of the French language, I said I had never heard of that religion before. He smiled at me, and then it was his stop and he had to go. My companion nudged me and said in her broken English, "Muslim. Muslim, Sister Smart."

Wow, I felt like an idiot. I never again forgot what that word sounded like. Of course, I'd heard of Islam. I didn't know tons about it, but I had a friend in junior high who was Muslim. We didn't spend a lot of time discussing religion, but I had learned through association that Muslims believed in Allah, that Muhammad was their greatest prophet, and that — like Mormons — they valued family and modesty. It seemed to me that Mormons and Muslims had something else in common: People who don't know anything about the actual tenets of our faith are quick to judge us based on the actions of a few fringe extremists. All that said, as part of our training, we were taught that we should not proselytize or attempt to convert Muslims, recognizing that, depending on their country of origin, they might face terrible repercussions for even contemplating another faith.

My mission was one of the hardest yet most rewarding experiences of my life. I learned so much about my own faith, other people's faith, other religions, a whole different culture and language, and I learned a lot about human nature as well. There are some people who are going to hate you for no reason other than that you are there, talking about religion. But you also meet some of the kindest people in the world.

One of the people who made a lasting impression on me was a native French-woman named Giselle, who lived in Caen with her two small children. She invited my companion and me into her small apartment and started telling us about her life. She cared about everyone and everything and truly practiced the "love thy neighbor" teachings of her Christian faith. She told us that years earlier, as she prepared to go on vacation, she noticed a homeless person who was a regular outside her apartment building. That day, instead of rushing by and ignoring that person, she stopped and said, "I live on the sixth floor. Here is my key. Stay here as long as you need to." When she got back to her apartment after her vacation, there was nothing left. All her belongings — furniture, clothes, food — everything was gone. Instead of reporting the robbery to the police, she sighed and said, "Oh, well. They needed it more than I did anyway." And she started over with nothing but the contents of her suitcase.

If my mission and my religion have taught me anything, it's that faith isn't just what you believe in; it's how you live, how you love, and how you move forward.

My faith — and this religion that's been the vehicle for my faith — has played a huge role in my life. It's always been there for me when I needed something to hold on to. At the end of the day, if all religions prove to be wrong, I won't regret believing, because it has made me a better person and has helped me live my life in such a way that I will never need to be ashamed of any part of it. I think most religions are that way: a set of beliefs that help provide hope, healing, and a meaningful way of life. It really is something quite beautiful and extraordinary, if you take the time to stop and think about it.

However, there are those who are willing to sink so low as to take those beautiful beliefs and ways of life and twist them and manipulate them until they no longer resemble what they should. Every religion on the planet has seen that infected sliver: a self-serving extremist fringe that has nothing to do with faith and everything to do with agenda. Brian David Mitchell and Wanda

Barzee are prime examples: two people who perverted Scripture in the ugliest, most self-serving way imaginable, using it to deceive and harm people. To harm a *child*. There couldn't be anything more despicable.

Because I was that wounded child, I felt a certain empathy when I recently heard the story of a little girl in Afghanistan.

As a child growing up in a war-torn country, this little girl (we'll call her Fatima to protect her privacy) was used to the sights and sounds of conflict. In her brief life, she'd already seen too much. She'd witnessed a relative who was heavily pregnant being killed by her husband for leaving the home without his permission. She often heard one of her uncles say, "It is better for a woman to be in the grave than to go to work and show up in public." Her family eventually fled Afghanistan. They lived as refugees in Pakistan for a time, then returned to their home country, hoping things might change. Inside and outside this little girl's home, there was a war zone in which a twisted version of their religion was used as a weapon against women — and against faith.

One day when Fatima was seven years old, she was working in the fields alongside her father. Suddenly, a huge explosion rent the air. Everything went black. When Fatima regained consciousness and opened her eyes, she saw her father and knew immediately that he was dead. When she finally was able to tear her eyes away from her father's body, she looked down and saw that her leg was badly mangled. Fatima was taken to the hospital, where the doctors amputated her leg just above the knee. This devastating moment turned out to be the beginning of a long, terrifying journey that shook her family to its foundation and galvanized a greater purpose in her life — a purpose made more powerful because it was guided by her faith.

When my friend Dana told me briefly about Fatima, I wanted to know more. I reached out to Fatima, but she was away celebrating Ramadan. *How long is Ramadan?* I wondered. *When will it end?* Early July. Thank you, Google. I waited until July and invited Fatima and Dana to come up to my home for lunch, hoping she would allow me to interview her for this book. In my experience, faith is an integral part of hope, and religion is a framework for faith, so I knew I had to ask about hers. I thought it was important to include in this book interviews with people whose religion is different from my own but whose faith has sustained them the way my faith sustained me.

When the day arrives, I want Fatima to feel welcome in my home. I generally don't do a great deal of cooking, and my cooking is nothing to get that excited about anyway, but I want this to be nice. Despite my best plans, the kitchen doesn't look as tidy as I want it, and there's no time to waste. I jump in my car, quickly strapping my trusty sidekick Chloé into her car seat, and off we go to Whole Foods. Personally, I love Whole Foods, but it's a bit trendy — and a bit spendy — for everyday living. It's more of a special-occasion grocery store for us. I know exactly what I want. Nothing heavy. Flaky, light croissants for chicken salad sandwiches, an array of cheeses and fruit for a cheese platter, some of the premade quinoa salads and kale salads, and a beautiful Chantilly cake loaded with berries for dessert. I quickly push my cart through the store, snatching things up as I go. Whenever we have people over for a meal, I always, without fail, overdo it with too much food. This time is no exception; I end up spending over a hundred dollars just on the cheese. I guess it's clear that France gave me not only a love for pastry but a love for cheese as well. Usually if you look in my pantry or fridge and we don't have much of anything, the one thing you are guaranteed to find is cheese.

Chloé, of course, decides she would prefer to be out of the cart rather than safely buckled in, so now I'm trying to push the cart and convince her to sit still. That usually means no one wins. Fortunately, I make it up to the checkout before the real struggling begins. I don't blame Chloé for wanting to get out and look at things and touch things. That's what I want to do every time I'm in Whole Foods!

Once we get home, I try to make everything look lovely and presentable. My mom is so much better at this kind of thing than I am. She has an artistic flair that shows in everything she does. Me — not so much. But I try. And somehow I manage to pull it off. It's probably the yummy Chantilly cake on the glass cake stand that elevates the presentation above my usual status quo. I want Fatima to feel my appreciation for her willingness to talk to me. This young woman has been through so much. The loss of her father and her leg to that land mine. The loss of her childhood to poverty and struggle. The loss of her peace and safety to misogyny and threats of violence.

My house is at the corner of two forked streets on a mountainside. There's no fence around my yard, so when I sit on my deck (where I have lunch set up), people can see me as they drive by, which can be confusing, because when I tell people my address, their GPS sends them to my front door and driveway around the corner. So today, as I'm adding the last-minute touches to our lunch on the deck, I look up and see a white sedan pull over to the curb and park. Two people get out, and one is my friend Dana, so the other must be Fatima. Instead of walking or driving back around to the front door, they hike down the grassy incline to my deck. I have a mini heart attack, thinking about Fatima's leg, but she doesn't hesitate for a second. She troops down the slope and climbs the steps to the deck with only the slightest limp.

"Hello." I offer my hand. "I'm Elizabeth. Thank you so much for coming."

Fatima looks me over carefully and says, "Dana gave me your book to read before we met. I thought you would be older."

"Really?" I have to laugh at that. "Usually it's just the opposite. People see me frozen in time as a fifteen-year-old."

We sit down and start to eat lunch, but Fatima hardly touches the food on her plate.

Maybe I'm just used to living with boys, I tell myself; whenever there's food around, it's gone in about half a second. Maybe she doesn't like American food. Maybe she's not hungry. Maybe she's too nervous to eat. Or maybe I'm too nervous about not offending her. *Why won't my brain stop worrying about how much she eats?*

I attempt small talk for a bit before I start peppering her with questions, but Fatima doesn't seem to be one for a lot of small talk. So I set out the digital recorder and dive in. Fatima's story tumbles out in bits and pieces. I'm going to paraphrase here rather than quote her directly. I want to be clear, because the story is so important.

The loss of a leg would be trial enough for anyone, but the death of her precious father was devastating to Fatima and her family. His death meant more than just the loss of a beloved family member; it meant the loss of their income, the loss of their freedom. They had to move in with an uncle who was cruel and abusive to Fatima, her mother, and all her siblings. Her trouble did not end there; Fatima's family learned that the explosion was the result of a mine specifically targeted at them. The Taliban had found out that her father was working against them. Even after his death, they

164

continued to target Fatima's family and extended family, to make an example of them. Life became unbearable, and they had to relocate back to Pakistan for their own protection.

Fatima, her mother, her five sisters, and her one brother lived all together in one small room in the home of a relative. Fatima's mother took in sewing to make a little extra money to send Fatima to school to get an education, though her uncles and aunts didn't want her to go and living conditions made it virtually impossible for Fatima to study. Despite all this, Fatima loved learning and school. Imagining a better life for herself and her family, she applied herself to studying and taught herself to speak English.

Fatima's mother was still a young woman, so her brothers hoped to marry her off again, but Fatima's mother refused. She wanted to give her children the best odds for survival, and she felt that if she remarried, she would be destroying any chance of that. She also knew that she was dying. Fatima's mother had been diagnosed with brain cancer, but she didn't tell her children until the very end, six months later. She didn't want them to worry about her. She died clinging to the hope that Fatima would go to school and get a good job to help support her siblings.

Fatima did just that. She graduated from high school and returned to Afghanistan in search of a job. She found work with a private contractor in Kabul, then went on to work as a translator for a military base. As she struggled to build a career with which she could support her family, she became more and more frustrated with the discrimination continually shown toward women. She made the bold choice to go to work for Oxfam International, teaching and promoting women's rights in different communities. Fatima also continued her schooling and ultimately did her thesis on women's rights.

Having accomplished all this, Fatima traveled to Jalalabad, to one of the districts where her family originated, to visit the grave sites of her parents. It's the custom there, when one visits a family grave site, to pass fruit out to the people around, so Fatima thought nothing of it when a small boy approached her. But instead of fruit, he handed her a sealed envelope, telling her, "There's a letter for you from that man." Fatima looked up and saw a tall, bearded man with a turban wrapped around his head. She didn't recognize him, so at first she thought the letter must be for someone else. Surely it could not be for her. But it was. When she opened it, she found a letter from the Taliban threatening her if she did not stop working for foreigners and women's rights. Knowing all too well how serious this threat could be, Fatima made the very difficult decision to leave her family and everything she knew. She came to America, seeking asylum, and Dana took her in.

Trying to process all this, to make sense of the bits and pieces, I take a deep breath of the cool mountain air before I ask her the question so many people have asked me. "After everything that's happened to you in the name of religion, Fatima, do you still believe?"

"It's not the religion that makes people good or bad," she says. "Mostly it's the culture. For instance, Islam never says to kill a woman because she goes out and works. In fact, it encourages people to go out and work and gain an education. The wife of Muhammad the prophet was an entrepreneur. How could Islam start from these things? The bad things like killing, stoning, beating, and abusing are a misinterpretation by *people* — people who use Islam for their own benefit."

"Fatima, how has your faith helped you?"

"I pray to God a lot. Whenever something terrible is happening to us, whenever we are in extreme situations, I always pray to God, and my prayers are answered. I did not think it would be possible for me to come to America, but I prayed a lot. My sisters prayed a lot. And I was able to come."

I also believe in prayer. I have for as long as I can remember. When I was little and my parents would tuck me into bed at night, they would often share stories from their childhoods. Sometimes Mom would tell us about family road trips when she and her eight brothers and sisters would climb into the dependable station wagon with her parents in the front seat — her dad at the wheel, her mom as navigator with the trusty map — and they would set out for an adventure. They'd go to the beach or a lake, or if they were really lucky, to Disneyland. Occasionally they would go all the way up to Canada and visit Banff.

On one of their adventures, somewhere out in the middle of the desert, they missed the last turnoff to refuel and continued on, thinking, *We'll be okay. We can make it to the next service station.* They even tried a shortcut. But they didn't find a gas station.

The family car, with its dying chug, made it to the top of a hill. Grandpa said, "We'll coast down this hill, but after that we can't go any farther without more gas." He took his foot off the brake, and they coasted down the hill, stopping a little distance away. I can only imagine the squabbling that went on then. My mom has never said anything about that, but I have been on enough road trips and had enough car troubles to know that those two things put together add up to a perfect recipe for short tempers and plenty of complaining. Eleven people in the same car, no AC, stuck in the middle of the desert. Sounds kind of like hell.

My grandparents remained calm, and a family prayer was said. They asked God for some fuel to make it to a gas station. Shortly after they completed their prayer, to their surprise a big truck came barreling down the hill and slowed to a stop next to them. The window was slowly cranked down, and a man's face appeared. The man asked, "What seems to be the problem?" My grandpa told him what had happened. The man smiled and said he had plenty of gas with him. The trailer he was towing behind his rig happened to be full of gas. He whipped out a hose and a nozzle and filled the station wagon's tank not partway but all the way with gas. Before he left, my grandpa tried to pay him, but he wouldn't accept even a penny. Almost as suddenly as he had appeared, he was back in his truck, trundling off down the highway. To some this story may seem like it was just luck, or it was coincidence, or the good deed of a fellow human, but I believe that it was a miracle, an answer to prayer — and that's not the only small miracle I've seen or heard of in my life.

When I was a little girl in Sunday school, I looked up to my teacher, Jane Hinckley, for her bright smile, intelligence, and strength of spirit. She's a bit younger than my grandmother, but she has youthful energy, plays tennis and guitar, and always wore a particular shade of coral lipstick. Sister Hinckley is married to Elder Richard G. Hinckley, who comes from a long line of influential Mormons. His late father was the Mormon prophet President Gordon B. Hinckley. Elder Hinkley has known my family for many years. I remember going over to my Sunday school teacher's house and seeing him there when I was little. Elder Hinckley is a general authority, which means he is assigned to do different tasks by the first presidency (our prophet and his two counselors). He always has a smile on his face and a twinkle in his eye. As someone who has known me my whole life and traveled the world in the name of religion and met with world leaders, he came to mind as a great person to interview.

The Hinckleys live in Salt Lake City, not too far from the home I grew up in. As I drive into town, I keep the windows up and the AC on. The temperature must be in the high nineties if not the low hundreds. Stepping out of my air-conditioned car is like stepping into a sauna — and not a good one. It's just a couple yards to their front door, thank goodness. I glance back at my black car, which is only partially shaded by the trees that line the sidewalk, thinking, *Well, that thing is going to be an absolute inferno when I come back out.* Oh well. Not a whole lot I can do about that now. Like a lot of things in life, you just have to let it be what it's going to be and do your best to tough it out when the time comes, knowing that the trip will have been worth it.

I knock on the door, and the friendly face of my old Sunday school teacher appears. Jane smiles and holds the door open, smiling. "Elizabeth! So good to see you!" She asks about my parents and siblings as she leads me through to the living room. Elder

Hinckley strolls in, and we sit down on adjacent sofas, catching up a little bit. Then I set up my recorder and consult the list of questions I've prepared.

"What has been your experience in regard to faith and hardship?"

"I think everyone has different experiences with faith and hardship," he says. "I think for me, probably the most significant experience in my life in that regard was about eleven years ago when I injured my right eye. Ultimately, it cost me my vision in that eye, but I was with my father. He was the president of the Church, and he'd invited me to accompany him on an around-the-world trip. He was ninety-five and in great health. We were scheduled to first go to Anchorage, then Vladivostok, Russia, and then Korea, and Taiwan, and India, and we dedicated a temple in Aba, Nigeria, and so on and so forth — several other stops. I got as far as midway between Anchorage and Vladivostok across the north Pacific and was standing up in the airplane with an exercise band under my foot. The plastic handles were both in my right hand, and I had it fully extended when it slipped out from under my foot and hit my eye, and everything went black in that eye."

It never ceases to amaze me just how

fragile we are as human beings. In the blink of an eye, literally, the scene flashes from "everything's fine" to "everything went black."

"Did you realize immediately how seriously you'd hurt yourself?" I ask.

"It was extremely, extremely painful," Elder Hinckley says, nodding. "Fortunately, we were able to turn around and get back to Anchorage. Long story short — in terms of faith and trial — I spent the next seven weeks in surgeries and in bed in a darkened room, unable to read or watch television or do anything. A lot of time. A lot of pain. A lot of nausea. But a lot of time to think. It was very interesting for me, Elizabeth, because after a couple of weeks of that, everything in your life boils down to very simple, basic things. Everything, you don't care about — your bank account, your stock brokerage accounts — you don't care about the car you drive or the house you live in. What you care about is your family, and the Lord, and the gospel, and the eternal nature of marriage and family, and nothing else matters. *Nothing* else matters."

"When you prayed then, did you ask to be healed? Or for the pain to go away? Or . . . ?"

"I remember during those seven weeks in bed praying a lot. *Heavenly Father, please, bless me that — Teach me whatever I need to know. Because I don't want to go through this again, so whatever it is I need to know . . .*" He raises one hand and clarifies, "Now, it wasn't anything like your experience, clearly, but for me it was life-changing. It really was, because you had all that time, and you were suffering, and everything just fell away like the refiner's fire, and the dross falls away. You're just left with a few nuggets of pure gold. That's the gospel, and eternal life, and eternal marriage and family, and that's it. Nothing else mattered."

"Have you ever felt you can't continue?"

"I'll go back to that accident — and I think it was the pain I was in and the nausea I was suffering — but there were times when . . . I'm just embarrassed to admit that . . . Maybe I shouldn't say it."

I don't interrupt him, but I lean in a little, trying not to let him see that I want him to say it, whatever it is.

"I was wishing I would die," he says. "I just didn't want to go through that any longer. I was pretty sedated, but I had a lot of time when I was conscious enough to think and to pray. And so you do. I did turn to prayer a lot. I think we all do. I think that's the key. You turn to the scriptures, you turn to prayer, you turn to your wife or your husband, and trusted friends whose faith will strengthen yours. You're never alone. Even if you're on an island alone — or in your former situation where you were *really* alone — you still had prayer, and you still had your faith. So you're never quite abandoned. That's what you have to exercise: faith and prayer and patience. Patience is sometimes the hardest thing of all. Saying, 'This too shall pass.' "

Elder Hinckley points out the obvious here, that patience is sometimes the hardest thing of all. For me, patience doesn't come naturally, but the older I've gotten, the better I've become at waiting.

When I was kidnapped, I would pray every day that somehow someone would find me, or that I would find a way to escape, or that my captors would go into a coma, or whatever. Well, none of these things happened in the way I imagined them happening. Each day seemed to stretch on for eternity until it seemed that the majority of my soul had shut down and only the minimum was running on autopilot through the days and nights. Nights were easier, because I could escape into my dreams and no one could hurt me there. As the days dragged on, my spirit and hope faded. How could I keep going? All my prayers seemed to go unanswered. Or were they unheard? I didn't know. I just felt lost, alone, and scared.

It was summer, and the heat was almost unbearable. The trees that surrounded the hideaway seemed to do nothing to keep the heat out. Even the shade was hot. Because we were high on the mountainside — and not to be indelicate, but this camp didn't exactly have indoor plumbing — water was very hard to come by and had to be used very sparingly. I wasn't allowed to make the hike down to the nearby stream. Only Mitchell went to this place where cool, clear water bubbled out of the ground. Barzee was always left behind on guard duty. The water would be retrieved in empty gallon milk containers, and then the containers would be put into two separate green army bags, which would then be tied together with a navy blue sash. The bags would be slung over Mitchell's shoulder, one bag in front, and one bag in back. It was tricky getting back to the hideout with the water because the mountainside was so steep and the vegetation unfriendly for the most part. So it wasn't something that Mitchell relished doing. He should have thought about that before he kidnapped me.

Finally, there was a day when we ran out of water. The night before had been hot and felt humid. That morning, I was so thirsty, I went through all the containers hoping for a few drops of water. But they were bone dry. It was another scorcher that day. I asked Mitchell if he planned on going back down for water.

He looked at me and said, "No."

Even Barzee asked him if he would go down for water. He told her he didn't feel it was safe to wander out to get water because there were too many searchers in the area. He didn't want to leave any tracks.

We went to sleep yet again with dry throats. I had a very difficult time falling asleep that night, which was far from the norm. Usually, as soon as I lay down, I would fall asleep. I prayed to my Father in Heaven, asking for some relief. *I'll take it in any form. Just please help me.* I finally fell into a fitful sleep. I don't remember if I had any dreams or not, but I wasn't sleeping well.

All of a sudden, I awoke. I was confused. It wasn't morning yet, wasn't light outside. Why was I awake? I looked around the tent. As usual, both Mitchell and Barzee were there by the tent door, guarding it even in their sleep. Then I noticed the small plastic cup we used every day. It was just above my pillow. How had it gotten there? I certainly hadn't brought it in. Last I'd seen, it had been outside with the other plates and cups. I reached for it, and when I picked it up, I realized it was full to the brim with ice-cold, delicious water. I immediately put the cup to my lips and began to drink. I could feel the cool liquid running down my throat and reviving my parched innards. To this day, that water was the best drink I have ever had. Although that simple cup full of water wasn't someone there to rescue me, or a yellow brick path to my home, it was a sign to me. It was my Heavenly Father's way of telling me that He knew where I was and what I was going through, and He had not forsaken me. I had to have faith and patience and keep surviving and somehow, someway, I would find my way home to my family again. Finding the cup filled with water wasn't the only miracle or tender mercy I experienced while I was kidnapped, but it is one of the most sacred for me. I do not speak of it very often because it is so special to me. But it is true. It did happen, and I will never forget it.

Each one of us strives to find peace and happiness in this life, and we hope for a better future in the next. For me, my faith and my religion provide me with that peace and happiness. It's not always easy, and I have been asked how I would feel if I found out it wasn't true.

My answer is simple: It's my truth. It makes me a better person. If at the end of my life I die and find out it isn't true, I will have lived life being the best person that I can be — hopefully someone who is kind, compassionate, and patient. Knowing I will never regret my dedication to these ideals — that's what faith is for me. But I can't claim that this faith has never wavered or made me wonder. It's comforting to hear Elder Hinckley say the same is true for him.

"I struggled with my faith," he says. "Not terribly, but I had a lot of questions, particularly as an older teenager, prior to my mission and some after my mission, which was a German-speaking mission from 1961 to '63. We served two and a half years in those days, because there was no language training program, no missionary training center, so we just went, and that extra six months was intended to give us more language skills. I think my mission experience was very, very influential — along with the example of my parents, of course. I don't think I ever wavered or had any questions about the divinity of Jesus Christ or of his atonement, but the other things had to be fit into the jigsaw puzzle a piece at a time.

179

They're mostly all in place now, and those very few that are still questions are very insignificant. I have complete faith and hope that they'll be resolved and make sense when the time is right."

That faith in faith itself reminds me of Fatima's quiet sense of solid ground as she ambled down the hill behind my house. She can feel it with one foot; her other foot steps forward on faith alone. It's humbling sitting next to Elder Hinckley because of the extent of his education and the depth of his understanding, but I felt the same way listening to Fatima speak. Her understanding is based in experience — what's happened to her and what she's witnessed — and she's not afraid to claim her truth for herself and take strength from it. She is not loud or boisterous in any way. She's very calm and quiet. Many people might pass her by or think her nothing more than a simple wallflower. But she shows dignity and strength of character. There's something solid about her presence that you can't deny, even if you don't know that she's been tested beyond the limits few people ever face and has come through intact. Both she and Elder Hinkley are devoted to a faith that is easily misunderstood, but they practice their respective religions without apology, without getting distracted.

Mormons are often teased for our standards. We're often asked if we're allowed to have fun, why we don't do things on Sunday. We have a set of guidelines that we try to live our lives by. We believe that they are there to protect us. And trust me, if anyone knows how to throw a completely sober yet entertaining party, it is the Mormon Church. Mormons have been the subject of a Broadway musical and episodes of *South Park*. There are lots of jokes about Mormons, our beliefs, and how we act. A lot of them aren't exactly what you would call complimentary, but the following one makes me crack a smile each time I hear it.

There was a plane about to crash, and on that plane, there was a bishop (a lay minister whom you would consider the "father" of the congregation), a primary president (a sister in charge of teaching the children), and a high priest (another layman who meets with other high priests from the surrounding congregations to discuss different matters and dilemmas).

As the plane lost altitude, the high priest, who was notorious for giving long, dry sermons, got up and prayed, "Please, God, let me give one last sermon."

The primary president closed her eyes and

prayed, "Please, God, let me sing one last song."

"Please, God," the bishop prayed, "let us live long enough for the primary president's song and crash before the high priest can give his sermon."

It's funny, but in the end, maybe that's how religion and faith work together best: We take the song and leave the sermon; we cherish the faith of our fathers but decide for ourselves what resonates in our own hearts. And I think we must be clear with ourselves when we answer the simple, imperative questions:

What *do* I believe and how do I put my beliefs into practice?

Will my beliefs sustain me through life's refining fire?

Do they make me happy?

Do they bring me peace?

6
STRENGTH OF SPIRIT

Survival is not so much about the body, but rather it is about the triumph of the human spirit.

— DANITRA VANCE

Often people say to me, "I could never survive what you went through." Or worse, they say, "I went through some difficult experience — but of course, that's nothing like what *you* went through." It's not a competition. There's no prize for the biggest tragedy and no value in comparing our trials to the trials of others. I promise: You are stronger than you think you are. If you haven't been tested, you may not fathom that reservoir of inner strength, but I guarantee, there will be an occasion for you to rise to.

I first heard of Diane von Furstenberg when I was studying abroad in London. I shared a room with five other girls, two of them twins who were both into fashion — and not just trendy fashion. High fashion. We went to Wimbledon one day to explore the legendary tennis courts, and walking around the small town, we passed a boutique where both the twins were like, "DVF! We have to go in! I love DVF!" We walked into the boutique, and it was filled with beautiful clothes. Unfortunately, being a poor college student at the time, I could not afford a single item, but I looked at everything and left with some lovely things to dream about. I don't remember tons about the tennis courts, but I remember that boutique.

The more I learned about Diane von Furstenberg, the more fascinated I became with her and all she's been able to accomplish. I consumed her memoir, *The Woman I Wanted to Be,* which is exciting, full of life, color, and movement. When I finished reading it, there were three words that stood out in my mind describing her: love, freedom, and sexy. My admiration for her grew, and so did my admiration for her mother, who reminds me a lot of my own mom. Diane von Furstenberg is the daughter of an incredible woman, Liliane Nahmias, who was a prisoner at both Ravensbrück and Auschwitz. Liliane had been working for the Belgian Resistance, living in a safe house. It was her job to deliver fake documents and papers to those who needed them. When she was arrested, she was able to quickly scribble a note to her parents using a burnt match as a pencil. She told her parents she didn't know where she was going, but she was leaving with a smile on her face. Also on the note was a plea to anyone who found it to please deliver it to her parents. Her family did receive the note; Diane came across it years and years later, after her mother had passed away.

Liliane survived thirteen months total in both camps. When she was liberated, she weighed a mere fifty-nine pounds — barely the weight of her bones. Reading that struck such a chord for me. I could relate to that moment, though I was the opposite of emaciated when I was brought home, swollen from sunburn and bloated by malnutrition. But just as my mom cared for me in those joyful but difficult days of readjustment, Liliane's mother nursed her back to health. Liliane married and, though she'd been warned she wouldn't survive childbirth, she had her daughter and raised her up with an indomitable spirit. Diane von Furstenberg always attributes her strength to her mother, who told her, "By giving you life, you gave me my life back. You are my torch, my flag of freedom."

"I didn't used to talk nearly as much about my mother," Diane wrote in her memoir. "I took her for granted, as children do their mothers. It was not until she died in 2000 that I fully realized what an incredibly huge influence she had been on me and how much I owe her."

Those words resonated with me. Although my mother never was sent to a concentration camp or worked in the Belgian Resistance, she was and is a fighter in her own way, and she was instrumental in making me who I am today. My hope and dream for the future is that I can be as good a mother to Chloé as my mother was to me. I want Chloé to know that beauty isn't everything, that it's important to be kind, strong, independent, and intelligent.

My mom is the glue that held my family together through thick and thin, never more so for me than in the first few months after I was rescued.

The morning of March 12, 2003, started out cold and foggy. My captors and I had spent the previous week hitchhiking back to Utah. Two cops at a Burger King in Las Vegas had confronted us, and for a moment

I felt a surge of hope that I might be able to communicate something to them, but Mitchell talked his way out of the situation while Barzee gripped my arm, reminding me what would happen if I tried to scream or run. My family would be murdered, and it would be as if I had murdered them. As the cops walked away, I felt hollow and hopeless. It felt like forever ago that my captors and I had first started the trek in the blazing sun and heat. I remember feeling like I was dying of thirst, wondering if I would ever make it back to Salt Lake alive.

A truck driver picked us up and drove us all the way to Orem, Utah. When we arrived, it was late at night or maybe very early in the morning. He had stopped at a trucking lot where he was delivering his load and told us we had to get out. This was as far as he could take us. Mitchell, Barzee, and I jumped down from the semi. I was so tired I could hardly walk straight, especially with the heavy bags I was forced to carry. Mitchell led the way out of the lot where the semi was parked. As we approached the highway, I was barely aware of what was around us, but Mitchell pointed down the road a little ways and said there looked to be a place where we could hide out until morning.

We crossed the highway and entered a

park called "Camelot." It was all reminiscent of King Arthur and the round table. It seemed somewhat secluded and, most important, empty. We walked to the back of the park, and Mitchell set up the small two-man tent that all three of us squished into. I was so tired, I didn't even care about being smashed next to Mitchell. He had done so much to me already that this hardly seemed like anything. It must have been only a few hours later that he was shaking me awake, saying we needed to get up and get out of the park before it opened and people arrived. We quickly packed everything up and headed out.

When we were back out on the road again, a student picked us up and apologized that he couldn't take us farther but would drive us the couple miles down the road to a Mc-Donald's for breakfast. I was allowed to get an Egg McMuffin, which may not sound all that special, but at the time, having hardly eaten for several days, I thought it was mouthwateringly delicious. The past nine months had never been easy as far as food was concerned. More often than not, I went without, so having something warm and hot and full of flavor — something that hadn't come out of a garbage can — was a real treat.

After breakfast, we headed back out and slowly started making our way the fifty miles or so remaining into Salt Lake City. We took several different buses, and when questioned about who we were or why I was wearing a wig and sunglasses, Mitchell would make Barzee and me get off the bus and wait for the next one. Mitchell and Barzee were becoming more and more anxious the closer we got to Salt Lake. Mitchell said that once I was back at the hideout where they'd taken me the first night I was kidnapped, I wouldn't be allowed to leave again. I understood that he meant I was a prisoner who'd been given a life sentence — or a death sentence. Still, I was just so happy to be back in Utah. At least I would live or die here, close to my family, in this place I loved. I was intent on soaking up every possible moment of freedom I could.

We finally made it to the outskirts of Salt Lake. We went into a Walmart to "plunder" (steal) some essentials that we would need to survive in that original camp, including new hiking boots for all three of us. As we walked out of the store, I remember stopping at a bulletin board that had pictures of missing children on it, looking for my face, for my real name. I had only a brief opportunity to look at it before Mitchell grabbed my arm and pulled me away. He told me to stop drawing attention to myself *or else.* I knew what that meant, so I went along quietly, disheartened that I hadn't seen a picture of myself. *Have people stopped looking for me already? Do I not qualify to be on the bulletin board?* These were the thoughts going through my head as we walked out the door and continued on our way, heading back for the mountains on the northeast side of the Salt Lake Valley, in the direction of my home and my family.

We were heading north on State Street, barely out of the Walmart parking lot, when a police car pulled up, and then another and another. There seemed to be dozens of them, more than I had ever seen at once, and the officers were all jumping out of their cars and coming over to where we were standing. They began questioning Mitchell. Standing there in his shadow, I was terrified. I'd been warned many times that if I ever did or said anything out of line, he would kill me, kill my family. That was a very real threat for me; out of pure survival instinct, I did exactly as I was told. Up to this point, I had never seen my captors fail at something they had said they were going to do to me. They had kidnapped me, chained me up, starved me, abused me. He had raped me, and she had facilitated that. Mitchell had been stopped and questioned — even spent time in jail — but no one had ever intervened to protect me or my family. How could this time be any different?

But this time *was* different. The police were absolutely persistent in questioning my captors, and finally — *finally!* — one of the officers must have noticed or had a gut feeling that I was scared and unsure about talking to them with my captors being so near. So the officer separated me from them by a few yards and started questioning me alone. Feeling Barzee's eyes on me, fearing this would turn out the way it always did, I initially held to the cover story that I had been told to tell — that I was their daughter — though the struggle going on inside me was intense. The officer told me how much my family missed me, how much they loved me, and how no one had ever given up hope of finding me. It was only then that I was able to admit who I was. I whispered it, barely breathing, scared of what might happen if he didn't believe me. And for a moment, it seemed that my worst fears were coming true.

The officer turned me around and handcuffed me.

Now my breath was coming in short, hard gasps. *What? Why? No!* He placed me in the back of the police cruiser and left me there, terrified and confused. Why had he just told me how much my family loved me and missed me and then handcuffed me? No one spoke to me as I was taken to the police station in Sandy, where I was brought into a small, windowless room. They took the handcuffs off me and told me I could remove the disguise I'd been forced to wear. I did as I was told, removing the wig and sunglasses. No one told me what was going to happen next. Then they left me alone and closed the door.

I sat on the edge of the battered sofa, too dehydrated to cry, needing my mom. I just wanted my mom. My mind ran wild. Why hadn't they taken me home? Why wouldn't they let me call my parents? Why had I been handcuffed and treated like a criminal? I scrunched my toes inside the stolen hiking boots. Was I going to be sent to prison? Compared with where I'd been the last nine months, prison didn't actually sound that bad.

And then the door to this closet-like room opened, and Dad came bursting through it. He was across the room in an instant, hugging me, crying, and asking, "Elizabeth, is it really you?"

I was unable to answer. It was so abrupt; I think I was in shock. My throat closed, choking me. I was crushed by the reality of how much had changed over the last nine months. My dad looked older, exhausted and torn up. I knew he was seeing only a shadow of the girl I had been before. I was a young woman now. I had grown and matured. My body was bloated and malnourished. I was no longer the healthy kid I had been when I was kidnapped. My face was red and swollen. I'd been exposed to blistering sun, hard labor, and horrific abuse.

But it was over.

I started to realize that I was safe. I was with my dad, and he was going to protect me. He was never going to let anyone hurt me again the way those two people had hurt me the last nine months. Everything was going to be all right. And I could breathe again.

Amidst our hugging and crying, an officer poked his head in the room and asked if we would accompany him up to the main headquarters in downtown Salt Lake. We got into the back of his unmarked maroon car and headed up to HQ. While we were in the car, my dad pulled out his cell phone and called my mom. No doubt she would be frantic, scared for the worst, prepared for it to be nothing, hoping for the best; such a flurry of emotion and panic. When she answered, I could hear her voice, and it sounded so beautiful. How long had I tried to remember how she sounded? How long had I been desperate to hear just one word from her? She was my mother, and I needed her. I had always needed her. I always will need her.

Of course, like a sick cosmic joke, right as my dad passed me the cell phone, the dumb thing's battery died. Honestly, what a moment to have a dead battery! We made it to the police station, where I was led upstairs, and my mother was waiting for me there. She was standing when I entered the room. She was wearing black pants and a black shirt with white trim around the V-neck. Her hair was pulled back into a ponytail. There was no hesitation with her whatsoever. We both ran to each other and hugged. That moment did not last long enough. I didn't want her to ever let go again.

My brothers and sister were all waiting to see me as well, but in the midst of our reunion, the police interrupted us and said I had to be taken for debriefing. That part is a little bit vague in my memory, but I do remember that I was taken to a small room where I was questioned by an officer, and there was a woman there. In the meantime, my dad had called John Walsh from *America's Most Wanted* and told him that I had been found and the police were questioning me. John informed my dad that the police didn't have any right to do what they were doing right then. That was all my dad needed to hear to go ballistic on the police. I was immediately taken from questioning and reunited with my family again.

Then the rest of my family went home to wait while my mom and I were taken to the hospital, where I had an extremely thorough physical examination and a rape kit done. Mom sat with me through everything — the tests, the poking, the prodding — and even though I don't remember it, I learned later that she was there listening to the police "debrief" me at the station. She heard and saw it all. I can't bear to think how difficult that must have been for my mother, watching her daughter recount unspeakably awful things that had happened to her, being tested and checked out for all sorts of diseases, having every media outlet in the world desperate to snap a picture of her.

In the following days, weeks, and even years, Mom never once faltered. She has been a constant pillar of strength and support for me. Now that I have my own daughter, who is my absolute world, I can't imagine anything more painful than going through everything my mom went through with what happened to me, but never, not once, has she ever shown a sign of weakness. Never has she ever pushed me or my pain away, even for a second, to spare herself what I know she must be feeling. To some degree, I suppose we all have at least a little selfishness in us, and perhaps it has been selfish of me to think of myself first and not consider how she might feel — what she felt upon seeing me, knowing that a part of my life had been ripped from her.

Later, during the various hearings and long trial, Mom sat listening to testimony from doctors, specialists, attorneys, and other people — some sane and some not so sane — and then finally to me. Listening to me recount every little detail of how I was abused, raped, and mistreated for nine months. Listening without ever looking like she wanted to be somewhere else. She was there in each moment, standing strong for me. As I sat on the witness stand and said everything I had to say, I kept telling myself, *It doesn't matter how you feel. You have to do this. Just pretend to be someone you want to be like.* I'm ashamed to say I sat there thinking of Grace Kelly, Her Serene Highness, the Princess of Monaco. I didn't want to look like I didn't have it together or like the defense attorney had ruffled me in any way. It worked, but I really should have been thinking of Mom, not Grace Kelly.

That's what I thought about when I saw the title of Diane von Furstenberg's memoir: *The Woman I Wanted to Be.* I thought about a strong mother, a mother with spirit. That's the chord it struck.

Mom has never backed down from anyone or anything when it comes to her children. That being said, she has always wanted us to know how to work, to be independent, and to realize that if we want something bad enough, we'll find a way to get it. She is my ultimate role model. So when Diane von Furstenberg says about her mother, "I owe her so much, because she made me so strong," I totally get that.

Shortly after the trial of Brian David Mitchell came to a close, I returned to finish my mission in Paris, and while I was there, I received an invitation from Diane to come to New York, where she wanted to honor me — to present me with an award and a donation of $50,000 to a nonprofit of my choice. (It was with that money that my dad and I were able to start the Elizabeth Smart Foundation, whose mission statement is "Bringing hope and stopping victimization.") I was overwhelmed by her generosity and by the idea that this woman I so admired actually thought of me in this positive light. That was several years ago, but I felt hopeful that she'd remember me and be open to answering some of the questions I'd been pondering. I sent her an email, asking if she might consider speaking with me for this book. I was elated when she graciously made time in her crazy schedule for a conversation.

I'm at Lake Tahoe in California, because my college roommates — some of my very best friends in the world — decided we needed a reunion, and as fate would have it, the reunion was scheduled for the same weekend I'd scheduled an interview with the queen of a fashion empire. I want to sound confident when I talk to her. I want to sound like a woman without fears, asking deeply thoughtful questions. I'll admit I'm so nervous, I've hardly slept at all. During the night, I woke up more times than I can count. But now my phone call with Diane is only minutes away.

I read over my questions, hoping she won't be disappointed in me. I sit out on the deck, breathing in the cool morning air and looking at the giant trees surrounding me. I scroll through my contacts and hit Call. The phone is ringing. I sit, holding my breath. Diane answers with her distinctive voice — that rich, unmistakable accent — and suddenly, everything is fine. After all my stressing and worrying, Diane is warm, friendly, kind, and perfectly lovely. She immediately makes me feel at ease. Maybe she knows how nervous I am, but she talks like she's known me for a long time and we're just catching up.

She asks, "So what is the book about?"

"It's about healing, moving forward, surviving, not giving up."

"Well, my mother was a survivor, as you know," she says, "and so I was the daughter of a survivor. I met a very interesting woman, and she said that there are two types of survivors: the ones who did not die, and the ones who live. There will be those who will always remember and be the victim, and ones who just won't. You have to go on, you have to learn, and you have to heal. Resentment and holding on to the past is so toxic."

"Did your mother ever talk to you about how she survived the death camps?"

"Not in detail," says Diane. "I said, 'How

did you survive?' She would say, 'Well, you know — say it's raining. Just imagine it's raining, and you go in between the drops.' She wanted to protect me from the suffering. She clearly suffered a lot, and she clearly kept a lot of things inside that she never told me. You have a daughter, though, right? The most important thing you can ever give your daughter is to make her fearless and independent."

I smile, thinking there's probably nothing I could do to stop Chloé from being fearlessly independent.

"Do you think your mother's spirit was ever broken when she was in the death camps?"

"She really wanted to survive. There's something about survivors that is very unique. She was different after, though. My father said that when he saw my mother again, when she came back, he didn't recognize her. She was a whole different person. He was taken aback because he left a happy, innocent girl, and found a broken woman, so to speak. She noticed it, and she said, 'You don't have to marry me,' and he said, 'No, no, I will.' But I don't think she was ever the same again."

When I think of Lily returning from the camps, a weakened shadow weighing less than sixty pounds, to find that the man she loved still loved her, I think of a line from my all-time favorite book, *Jane Eyre* by Charlotte Brontë. There is a part in the book when Mr. Rochester is speaking to Jane very passionately, and he says, "Whatever I do with its cage, I cannot get at it — the savage, beautiful creature! If I tear, if I rend the slight prison, my outrage will only let the captive loose. Conqueror I might be of the house; but the inmate would escape to heaven before I could call myself possessor of its clay dwelling-place. And it is you . . . I want: not alone your brittle frame."

Brontë so beautifully stated what it means to be a strong spirit trapped inside a body that is small and subjected to bullying and abuse. Mr. Rochester describes eloquently what each of us possesses inside. Our bodies are not who we are; our bodies can be destroyed, but the "wild, free thing" that resides in each of us is our spirit, the essence of who we truly are. I love this moment in the book so much. It confirms to me that horrible things can happen to us, to our bodies — including death — but even that does not destroy us. It simply frees our spirit.

I'm curious to know if Diane — who is so strong herself — attributed that strength to the fact that she had a strong mother. "Do you think people are born strong," I ask, "or do you think it's something that develops inside them as they grow? Or do you think it's something that they just have to develop in the moment?"

Diane hesitates for a moment and then says thoughtfully, "I think it's a combination. I think that a lot has to do with the way you were educated. That's why another important thing to give your child is health, and make them understand that they have to be their own best friend, because anything can happen, and they may only have themselves."

I ask Diane to tell me more about a moment she mentions in her memoir. She was traveling with her son and her mother when the airplane hit some turbulence. Diane says she wasn't really scared, but she had a momentary pang of unsettled nerves. She looked to her son and then to her mother, and the thought entered her mind: *Whose hand do I hold? My big strong son's or my frail and aged mother's?*

"You turn to your mother's hand instead of your son's hand."

"Yes, that said it all," she says. "I love that. I remember that, because my son was big and strong, and my mother was at her most fragile, back from the hospital, tiny and all of that, but it is her hand that gave me strength, yes. I love that too, because it was so eloquent, and it explained so much. I don't think she knew why I held her hand at the time, but it was so clear in my mind. I remember thinking, *Okay, where do I go for this strength?*"

"When your mother died, was it hard for you?"

Diane surprises me when she answers, "No, not at all. I barely cried, because she gave me all she could give me. I don't know. Sometimes I miss her, but she's there — her strength, she gave it all to me. There was nothing unresolved. Although it's after she died that I discovered how much of a huge influence she was for me and how much she was actually my role model. While she was my mother, and especially since she was so strong, you don't accept it. Her presence and her existence gave me a lot of strength."

Thinking of my own mother and what she means to me and of the strength Diane's mother instilled in her, I ask, "Have you ever been surprised by your own strength?"

"In Belgium, in my country, when I was growing up," says Diane, "everybody looked like you. They were pale, beautiful, with blond straight hair, and I was this little dark, curly-haired girl, and I looked like nobody. It's not that I liked what I looked like at all. I was fascinated. My mother had a big vanity in her bedroom, and I would spend hours looking at myself and making faces to myself. Once again, it's not that I liked what I looked like, but I liked that I had full control. Like if I would smile, she would smile. If I make a face, she would make a face. Somehow it's from that moment on that I realized that one has control over oneself, and total control over oneself, and therefore you can make yourself do whatever you want to do. I didn't look outside for strength. I didn't look outside for control. Somehow I find it inside. That doesn't mean that sometimes I don't feel sad or I don't feel insecure, even to this day. Now as I'm aging, it's a different moment of my life. I'm sixty-nine, and so I have moments of *Am I still relevant?* and all that. Nevertheless, sometimes you indulge yourself in being insecure, but when push comes to shove, then I am in charge. When you hear news about your health or anything, when it's a real problem, then you just say, 'Okay, deal with it.' "

There is so much to be said about being strong, finding your inner strength, but our time is limited, so I cut to the chase. "How do we protect and grow that inner strength?"

"By not lying to yourself. Ever," she says with certainty. "By not being delusional. By always saying the truth. By practicing the truth."

Listening to Diane speak so straightforwardly, openly, and plainly, I feel refreshed. It's as if a bit of her bold certainty has rubbed off on me. "Do you think there is anything about society today that inhibits the development of the survivor mentality?"

Again, her answer is brief and pointed: "Self-indulgence. I mean, people blame something for everything — their parents, the weather, something. It is never their own fault. The truth is, things happen. You can't blame anyone else for it, it just happens. You have to accept it and deal with it."

When she says "accept it and deal with it," it doesn't strike me as harshly as it does when I see it on paper. I think I get what she's saying: that things happen, and when they do, it's important for us to accept the fact that we can't change something that has already happened. So we need to move forward. That's all we can do. And moving forward might mean many things — counseling, professional help, forgiving, exercise, self-expression — but whatever form it takes, it simply means you make the best choice for yourself and do what you need to do to successfully continue to move forward.

"I want women not to be afraid of their own strengths," Diane says. "I have never met a woman who is not strong. Women are stronger than men, but they hide it so well. Sometimes because of a past relationship. Or often, because they don't want to show it because it's not feminine. In the face of tragedy, I'm always amazed how women take over. My advice is, don't be afraid of your own strength. Let it out. That doesn't mean you have to be less attractive, less feminine, or less anything. I think strength is actually very becoming. Having said that, it's not like you must feel strong all the time, but I want to be remembered as the somebody who told women, 'You can be the woman you want to be.' "

Diane von Furstenberg has become the woman she wanted to be. She overcame trials and setbacks and came out on top. Her strength and determination remind me of another strong determined woman who came from a background that couldn't be any more different than that of Diane's.

At a very young age, Mariatu Kamara was

sent away from her parents and her village in Sierra Leone to live with her father's sister, Marie, and Marie's husband, Ali. It is not uncommon for men to have multiple wives in Mariatu's culture, and when Mariatu was eleven, a man from the village approached her uncle, wanting to make Mariatu his second wife. Her aunt and uncle consented, but Mariatu was horrified at the thought. When she tried to tell her aunt that she did not want to marry this man — that he was a bad man and she hated him — her aunt slapped her and told her it was wicked to speak ill of her uncle's friend, her future husband.

This was during a time when civil war had broken out in Sierra Leone. Rebels would go through villages slaughtering people and destroying homes. The rebels hadn't yet come to her village, but many nights Mariatu and her cousins would be rushed to hide in the nearby jungle. After months of this, it finally happened: The rebels came, and Mariatu and her family fled to another village. When Mariatu and a couple of her cousins were sent back to retrieve food for her family, she and everyone with her were caught by the rebels. Mariatu recalls horrors most of us can't ever imagine seeing. People were forced into huts that were then set on fire. Little Mariatu watched as a woman and her small infant were forced into one of these huts. When the woman tried to escape out the window, she was shot in the head and fell back into the burning hut with her baby. Mariatu was petrified with fear.

The rebels killed many people around her, but when they came to Mariatu, they didn't shoot her. Initially, they planned on bringing her along, but ultimately they decided against it. But they said she couldn't leave unpunished. They asked her, "Which one first?" She didn't understand what they were asking — or that they weren't just taunting her. They gripped her little arm, hacked off her hand, and then gripped her other arm and hacked off the other, leaving her bleeding and helpless. Miraculously, Mariatu survived, stumbling alone through the jungle to the nearest town. She made it to Port Loko, where humanitarian aid workers arranged for her to be transported to Freetown to get the medical attention she needed. When Mariatu was eventually reunited with her cousins and her aunt and uncle, she found that her cousins had endured the same fate: They'd all lost their hands to the rebels.

While Mariatu was in the hospital, one of

the nurses who helped her bathe noticed her swollen breasts and asked her when she'd last had her period. Mariatu didn't know. She'd started menstruating just recently. The nurse's thorough examination revealed that Mariatu was pregnant. The nurse asked, "Who did this to you, Mariatu?" But Mariatu didn't know how it had happened. She hadn't learned yet how babies are made. But she told the nurse that the man who had wanted to marry her had found her home alone one day. He had pushed her to the ground, pulled up her clothes, and hurt her. Afterward, he had told Mariatu not to tell anyone what had happened.

Mariatu was still a child herself when the baby was born, but she struggled to care for the infant, living in the refugee camp with the rest of her family, begging for food on the streets. Mariatu's baby did not survive the harsh conditions of the refugee camp, but Mariatu was eventually able to get to London, and from there, she made it to Canada, where she built a life for herself.

Mariatu's circumstances and story are so compelling. She wrote about her experiences in a book called *The Bite of Mango,* and while her story is a world apart from the story told in *The Woman I Wanted to Be*

— the two are polar opposites in many ways — Mariatu embodies everything Diane von Furstenberg says about survival. She has never blamed anyone else, she has never let her lack of hands stand in her way, and she has never tried to hide her unbelievable strength and courage.

It took me a while to track her down and set up an interview, but the first time I talked to her on the phone, I was taken aback by how relaxed she was. She was happy to help and didn't think twice about talking to me. I was thrilled. I thought so much about the questions I wanted to ask her, and I reread *The Bite of Mango* to prepare for the interview.

The day of the interview, I feel like an absolute idiot, because I've chipped one of my front teeth and started panicking.

"My smile isn't even," I moan to my friend on the phone. "My face is ruined."

"Can you get it fixed right away?" she asks. "What do you have going on today?"

I tell her that I'm about to interview a remarkable woman who has survived civil war, rape, having her hands chopped off with a machete, losing a child, living in a refugee camp, and being separated from her family for the chance to seek a better life in Canada — which makes me shut up very quickly about my poor tooth. I'm thoroughly humbled, and that rapidly puts me in the mind-set of realizing how blessed and fortunate I am, and that I have nothing to complain about.

When it's time for the interview, I dial Mariatu's number, but she doesn't pick up right away. I count the rings, forcing myself to stop running my tongue over the edge of the broken tooth. The phone rings so many times that I wonder if maybe Mariatu has forgotten or perhaps changed her mind. And then I find myself wondering how she *does* answer the phone. It doesn't feel like an appropriate thing to ask, but my curiosity about it lingers, as irksome and persistent as that jagged little edge so close to the tip of my tongue.

When she answers, Mariatu is low-key and plainspoken, and I ask in the course of opening small talk what's going on in her life now.

"I was in school," she says, "but I decided to put that on hold while I do some public speaking to promote my book. And I am a UNICEF special representative for children of conflict."

This strikes me as an important calling for a little girl who experienced so many horrors. "Do you ever have nightmares?" I ask. "Do you ever feel scared?"

"Sometimes. Once in a while. Not all the time, but once in a while, yes."

"What do you do to help yourself feel better?"

"I just think positive. Staying on the good side. I continue on my forgiving path. There's not really anything special I do to make those memories go away. I just think positive and look forward. It will be a better road for me."

She goes on to tell me where this began for her: on that terrible road through the jungle when she was a little girl.

"I was just positive and hopeful that I would find help. When they cut off my hands, I was in the middle of nowhere. I didn't even know where I was going. With the help of God, I was able to survive that jungle and get to the hospital. My faith was very strong that I was going to survive, that I was going to live; I just didn't know how."

I suppose that's the definition of faith, in a way: to know, *I'll live through this, even if I don't know how.* So often the *how* comes first, and if we let it, that question can talk us out of our faith and undermine our strength. Let's face it: Some things just don't look good on paper. The scary statistics that confront someone diagnosed with cancer. The long odds of someone with a spinal injury ever walking again. We can't know what the future holds, but I like how Mariatu frames how we move toward that future: on a forgiving path, a better road.

"Do you feel that you've forgiven everyone who's wronged you?" I ask.

"Well, that's another thing I work on every single day," says Mariatu. "Each day, I wake up and have a second chance to see the world. There are things that can never be done in one time, in one day, one hour, or one year. It's just that you keep on working on it until you finally can grow out of it, so that's what I am doing. I am on the road of forgiving, I am forgiving them because there is nothing I can do about it. I mean, either I forgive them, stay positive, and have peace with myself, or still be bitter and not forgiving, leading me to become a horrible person — unhappy, unhealthy, miserable, and sad all the time. Crying over and over again. And I don't want to be like that. I want to be positive. I want to be a good example of a true survivor. I want to be strong for myself, and my family. I want to use that to inspire other people. That is why I am on the road of forgiving."

"What would you say to someone who's struggling to find that path?"

"Keep on fighting. Use what you have. Stop complaining," she says flatly.

Ouch. I feel that last admonition. "Yes. But not complaining — that's a challenge."

"Oh, I do complain sometimes," she readily admits, "but not out loud. Only to myself. I just try my best. Get up and do what I can to make myself happy. Make my life worth living. I don't give up. I *learn* to forgive, to be faithful to everything I do, and to stay thankful for the life I have. There's so many worse things out there that are going on."

That seems like a stunning statement from someone who's been through what she went through as a child. "When people meet you in person after they've learned your story, how do they react? And how do you react to them? Is there anything you want them to know?"

"I just wish that when people meet me, they won't feel pity for me, because I don't feel good when people pity me. I don't pity myself! I can do absolutely everything for myself. I live in an apartment with my four-year-old daughter. I just recently had someone join me, but I take care of my daughter, I take care of myself, I take care of the apartment, I cook, I clean — I do! You might not believe it, because you are not in my shoes. You might not understand exactly what I am capable of, or maybe you might have an idea. That's what I'm trying to say: that some people might see you and judge you right away, like, 'Okay, she's now a very dependent person' — but no, I'm not. I wish people wouldn't judge me or see me as less of a person or less of a capable person just because of my physical appearance."

I stand in complete awe of Mariatu. I have never met her face-to-face, but right now I can't imagine ever thinking of her as less than the hero she is. I do not pity her. I feel sorrow for the overwhelming amount of pain that's been heaped upon her, but I will always regard her with respect. To me, along with Diane von Furstenberg, she is the very definition of *strength of spirit.*

I can feel our interview is almost at an end. In the background, I hear Mariatu's daughter vying for her mother's attention.

Mariatu's tone changes when she speaks to her little girl. "Okay, pumpkin." She's a proud warrior on behalf of children in a terrifying world, but there in her kitchen, she's soft-spoken and warm, a mommy, just like me. Perhaps there is time for one last question, and as I have a daughter and I can hear her daughter, I ask, "What do you want for your little girl?"

"I wish and pray she will grow up and be the person God wants her to be," Mariatu says. "I want her to learn to respect people, be less judgmental, and be kind, caring, and understanding."

I am a little surprised that her answer is so simple, though maybe I shouldn't be, considering who Mariatu is. I guess I thought she was going to say something like, "To go to college, be successful, be happy, not have to endure the same things her mother endured." But perhaps that's a sign of how much I still have to learn.

I'm reminded of something else Diane said: "At the end, my biggest source of pride is my children."

I believe Mariatu would agree. I certainly do.

At the very end of our conversation, Diane said, "I'm glad you're happy. My advice to you is to have another baby as soon as possible. My mother always said you look at the darkness — it's so dark — but the only way you could deal with the darkness is to look for a tiny little bit of light and then build around that, and then all of a sudden, the fog lifts and the light is so magical."

As I'm writing this, I have followed Diane's advice. I found my little light in the dark: Chloé. I have held on to her and loved her, and that light has grown, and now I'm pregnant with Matthew's and my second child, and I feel and see the light that is so magical.

7
Our Physical Gift

Real beauty isn't about symmetry or weight or makeup; it's about looking life right in the face and seeing all its magnificence reflected in your own.

— Valerie Monroe

We have these amazing bodies that comport our spirits and take care of us, and we should be grateful for what we have, even if we're not as skinny as Victoria Beckham or as powerful as Beyoncé. Our bodies are to be celebrated, despite our individual limitations. Dressage has extended the capabilities of my body along with my understanding of my own strength. There are lots of styles of horseback riding; dressage is like yoga and ballet with military precision in partnership with the horse. You have to be very aware and in control, not only of your own body but of the horse's too, as best you can. Horses don't care if you're popular or pretty. When you get up on their backs, it's a dangerous position to be in. You have to control this thousand-pound animal, and for girls who come from a traumatic background, this is a really big confidence builder. This powerful animal knows nothing about your problems. You are in charge. It amazes me that this huge, powerful animal will allow us to get up there and take control.

For me, it all started because of my dad. A few years ago, he was looking for doors in the local classifieds, came across some for sale, and made an appointment to go see them. While he was looking at the doors, the seller's wife came out and saw my dad and realized that he was a relative. My dad asked her what she did for a living and found out she was a horse trainer at a local barn in Heber City, Utah. When my dad got home that evening, he called me and said if I was ever interested in taking dressage lessons, I had a second cousin not too far from me who taught professionally and would be happy to take me on as a student. I'd grown up spending a lot of time on horseback, but I'd never been instructed in riding — other than "Get up and stay up" — but I thought, *I'll give it a try. Why not? How hard can it be?*

Oh, how little I knew then.

I called and made arrangements to have a lesson. Let's just say this: Dressage is not easy. But I loved it. The feeling of being up on a horse is unlike anything else. For me, it feels natural and uncomplicated and helps me to step back and look at myself. But honestly, I wasn't doing much introspection during my lessons. I was constantly trying to remember everything: to keep my feet turned parallel to the horse's body, to keep my seat bones glued to the saddle, not to have too much tension on the reins, to feel the connection with the horse, not to cut the corners — the list could go on, but I'll leave it at that.

My weekly riding lessons became something I looked forward to. I was happy to get up early. I loved being the first one at the barn, grooming and tacking the horse, then being first out on the freshly groomed arena. It's a strangely satisfying feeling, being able to look back and see the shapes and designs you've made in the dirt while riding. (Also your mistakes.) I hadn't been riding at the barn too long when Annie, my trainer, suggested I consider getting my own horse. It didn't take much convincing. My whole life I'd dreamed of having horses of my own.

I started looking on all the different websites at horses for sale and found one not too far away that I thought looked promising. Unfortunately, despite being a very young horse, he had bad feet, the vet informed me, and would go lame very quickly if I rode him in training three to four times a week. So I continued searching. Annie and I even flew to California to look at some horses. While we were there, I rode a beautiful bay German Warmblood mare. She was simply magnificent. It took a lot of convincing for Matthew to finally agree with me that she was worth the money they were asking, even though I'd already talked down the price considerably. Anyone who owns horses can tell you that it's a black hole for your bank account; you will always put money into them, but you will never get a penny out of them. That being said, if you are bitten by the horse bug — and I don't mean horseflies — you know that you will happily continue to pay any amount because of the joy horses bring.

The deal finally closed, and I couldn't wait to get her shipped back to Utah. When she arrived at the barn that was to be her new home, she was the tallest horse there, standing over 17.2 hands. Every time I saw her, my heart swelled with pride. She was mine.

Her name was Bella, and in my mind, she was perfect. I was not a perfect rider, however, so there was a growing period for us — more for me than for her — but we came through it together. There's a saying in the horse world, "You ask a stallion, you discuss it with a mare, you tell a gelding, and you just pray for mercy from a pony." Bella and I did a lot of discussing.

I spent more and more time at the barn and began to know some people and make some friends. One person who made a strong impression on me was Lara Oles. She was so friendly and always had a smile on her face. She's a petite blonde, and I think I've seen her only once when she wasn't wearing riding attire. At first, I didn't even notice that one of her arms hangs at a slight angle and one of her legs has a slight drag to it. When I did notice, I didn't think much of it, because she was always right in there, grooming and getting her horse ready just like everyone else. Lara told me she had moved from Wyoming specifically to pursue her dressage lessons with Annie. She had initially begun with lessons at the National Ability Center in Park City, a place where people who have disabilities can learn to ski and horseback ride. It's called the Ability Center because the focus is on what you can do, not what you can't do. In fact, more often than not when I'm skiing in the winter, I see people wearing coats with the National Ability Center logo, and they're whizzing down the mountain so fast I don't have a prayer of keeping up with them.

Lara was driving about two hours both ways twice a week for a fifty-minute lesson at the National Ability Center. Then she found Annie. Lara and her husband decided to move to Heber City so Lara could pursue her dream, ride every day, and get all the training she needed. We shared a tack locker for a while, and as we got to know each other, I learned that Lara's angled arm and bum leg were the result of a skiing accident. Now she was training to compete on the world stage as a para-rider, maybe even a Paralympian one day. The first horse I knew with Lara was named Slate. He was a beautiful gray horse with a gentle look in his soft brown eyes. I was always impressed whenever I saw Lara ride him. He always looked so put together and seemed to anticipate her every command. No horse is perfect, but he seemed to be, despite a problem with a suspensory muscle and a few other ailments that required constant treatment and eventually a leave of absence.

Lara didn't know if she would ever be able

to ride him again, but to Lara, Slate was family. She took him home to live with her on her property, along with her two other trail-riding horses, a rescue mini horse, a rescue mini donkey, and her goats, chickens, dogs, and cats. If I were an animal, I would hope Lara could be my owner. She loves them and takes care of them to the bitter end. She began looking for another horse, and it didn't take long for her to find Bella — not my Bella, a different Bella in a barn down the road, but also a big beautiful bay mare. Actually, the two Bellas could have been twins. Lara didn't have a lot of money, but because of the immediate connection she had with Bella, the owner knew that Bella belonged with her. He turned down several better offers and chose Lara to be Bella's new owner.

Lara and I joked that we were now members of the "big bay mare club." Sadly, I didn't stay a member of that club for very long. Matthew and I had decided we wanted to have a baby, and soon after that I was expecting. Then my Bella got injured and had a very slow recovery, so we were both out of commission for a while. After my little Chloé Rose was born, I realized that I was at a crossroads. My Bella was and is a magnificent horse; she deserved to be ridden, worked, and shown. I knew that no matter how much I loved her and wanted to spend time with her, time with Chloé would always trump time with Bella, so I made the difficult decision to sell her.

I was very sad to see her go, but I knew it was for the best. And saying good-bye to Bella doesn't mean that I'll never ride or own horses again. Just not now. To everything there is a season. So for now, I live vicariously through Lara and her Bella on Facebook. Lara and Annie still invite me out for the occasional trail ride, which always makes my day.

When I think of people who are examples to me of courage, happiness, character, and determination, Lara always comes to mind. When I first emailed her to ask if she would be open to letting me interview her, she said certainly she would, but it took us a while to find a day that would work for us both, because she was competing in shows locally and internationally up in Canada.

But the day has finally arrived. I've been looking forward to talking with Lara and hearing firsthand how everything is going. All I see on Facebook is blue ribbon after blue ribbon being tacked onto Bella's bridle. My phone is suddenly buzzing, and I look down to see a text from Lara asking if I'd like to go on a trail ride after our conversation.

I answer, *Yes, please.*

That is what I think of as a perfect ending. I'm excited for our conversation, but I'm even more excited for our ride. I throw my beat-up old cowboy boots into the back of my car and drive the thirty minutes to Lara's house. In reality, I could have gotten there faster, but it's the kind of drive you're obligated to enjoy, winding between wooded hills and crooked trout streams. I pull up in front of Lara's log cabin home. Some of her horses are in the pasture behind her house, and her goats munch tufts of grass in their pen.

Lara welcomes me inside and asks, "Do you like to be cold or hot? It's hot up here, or we can go downstairs into the basement, and we'll be cool."

"We might as well be comfortable. Let's go downstairs." When we've settled in for our chat, I ask her one of those easy get-things-rolling questions: "Lara, how would you describe yourself?"

"Before my accident, I was a normal horse-crazy girl, but my accident transformed me into a competitive-crazed dressage queen."

"How did you start dressage?"

226

"It's always been more about the love of horses, not the love of competition. I never was really good enough at anything to be competitive, but I was born loving horses. My parents didn't even like animals. We grew up in Detroit, and I came out of the womb, 'horse, horse, horse.' I called dogs horses. I loved all animals, but horses were my soul being. My parents couldn't afford to buy me a horse, but they encouraged my love of horses and took me to lessons. Then once I learned how to ride, my mom's dear friend of a friend introduced me to this lady who let me ride her horses for free because I knew how to ride. I almost did have my own horses when I was a kid, but nobody had to pay for them except this rich lady. She was my fairy godmother. I used to go and just take off on these horses. I could take any friends I wanted and we'd go through the woods and through the orchards, down on the dunes, gallop along the beaches, and go swimming. I mean, talk about freedom — there were no fences and no 'No Trespassing' signs. It was all cherry orchards and open backyards. To the neighbors, I was just a kid on a horse, so they would just wave as I went by. It was ideal."

"How old were you when you had your accident?"

"I was thirty-nine," says Lara, who really doesn't look much older than that now.

"What happened?"

"I was skiing, and I fell. My right arm hit a post coming out of the ground. It was maybe seven or eight inches. I don't know for sure. Luckily, it wasn't any taller, because when my back-shoulder-arm area hit the post, it instantly unplugged my arm from my spinal cord. The three main nerves that run through your arm and connect to the spinal cord — the brachial plexus nerves at C7, C8, and T1 — they were just unplugged, like unplugging a toaster. My arm was instantly paralyzed. I knew it when I landed. When I quit sliding, I couldn't move my arm. I knew I had a spinal cord injury."

Lara calmly describes the devastating impact of the accident: ten broken bones, a punctured lung, and a bleed on the brain. A kind stranger skied over and offered to help her up, but even in the moment, Lara had the presence of mind to say, "No! I need to go down on a backboard. Call the ski patrol."

She tells me, "The doctors were like, 'Oh, you're really lucky. Your arm is bad. It's probably the worst-case scenario for paralyzing your brachial plexus and your arm permanently, but you're so lucky because you can walk. You should be really grateful. If that post had been any taller, you'd be dead or a quadriplegic right now.' Three days after my injury," she continues, "I got a blood clot on my spinal cord. And then I couldn't walk. It took several months of intense therapy before my leg could even bounce. It was like someone with cerebral palsy. It's taken more and more therapy, but I eventually made it to a walker, then a cane, then a really bad limp, and now sometimes I can fake that I don't have a limp at all. Because my arm is so much more noticeable, people don't even realize that my leg is bad."

But as she goes on, I begin to understand that the unseen effect of Lara's injuries are actually the most difficult to live with.

"I have lots of nerve pain akin to somebody who's had their arm amputated — and in some ways worse, because the pain is so close to my spinal cord. They didn't tell me this in the hospital, but when I read all the different studies on it, I learned this is one of the most painful nerve injuries you can get. The pain is really awful — like somebody is shoving a hot poker in my back or my wrist constantly. I'll be doubled over in pain rocking, screaming, and crying. I've finally found a medication cocktail that helps."

Listening to Lara describe the magnitude of her injuries, I think back to a day when I realized she had magnets that connected the bottom of her boots to her stirrups. *Must be nice!* I thought then, jealous that her feet were always held in the perfect position. Now that I get it, I don't envy those magnets at all.

When I ask Lara about the emotional impact of the accident, she says, "I woke up and I felt totally guilty, because it was a stupid accident. I blamed myself for that. I mean, accidents just happen, but I blamed myself because it was just dumb. I skedaddled, and I fell. I shouldn't have fallen. I felt guilty that my husband was going to have to take care of me the rest of my life. I didn't know if I was going to be able to walk again or what I was going to be able to do. The first thing out of my mouth to him was, 'Sell the horses.' We had just bought a brand-new truck, but I told Dan, 'Don't even bother.' We had put $400 down, but I thought, *We'll just eat it. Sell the horses. Sell the trailer. You're going to have a hard enough time taking care of me.* At that time, the doctors didn't know if my bladder and bowels were going to function because of my spinal cord injury. But Dan said, 'No. We're not selling the horses. You don't know what's going to happen in a year. You could be walking.' I tended to think of the worst — *I'm never going to ride again* — and I didn't want Dan to have to take care of me *and* my horses just to be nice. Dan repeated, 'We're not selling the horses.' He knew in his heart that they were my heart. They were the only thing to get me out of my funk. I would have withered away emotionally without something to work to get back to. He knew me better than I knew myself."

When Lara talks about her long road to recovery and how her horses made it possible, her posture takes on a tensile energy. She takes a conscious ownership of her body while most of us, I think, take it for granted that this arm, this leg, this hand will simply be there when we need it.

"At the time," she says, "I still felt like we should just sell them, but then I would go outside and pet them and I was happy we still had them. Horses are special. They have those big brown eyes that stare into your soul. They're so big, they could kill you with one kick, and yet, most of the time, they're willing to be with you. They put up with having able-bodied people ride them, but for them to be so forgiving and generous to take paralyzed people to the height of athletics of equine sport — it's really a miracle. They gave me a reason to get up in the morning. I could go out and hug them or just lie on them. When I was on them, I felt as normal as ever. I still feel more normal, more like my old self, when I'm on them. It's less limiting. They take me up into the mountains — and now into competition success. They are my legs."

Lara is passionate about her horses, what they have done for her, and what they have allowed her to feel and become. And again, there's that conscious ownership; she doesn't take that precious relationship for granted.

I ask Lara, "How did you deal with everything? Surely you felt anger?"

"Everybody has their own tragedies, right? I mean, I feel like I wear mine on my sleeve. Literally, people can see what is wrong with me, whereas people can't see what other people have gone through if it hasn't been physical trauma that can be seen on the outside. I think whatever happens to you — if you lose a husband, a child, or your innocence, or anything — it's a mourning process and part of that mourning process is anger. You have to go through those stages. I was raised by very loving and supportive parents, I have a loving and supportive husband, and they were able to help me through my accident and recovery. Then the animals — they give me what I call my warm fuzzies. They let me lie by them and feel their heartbeat and stroke their fur, and they look at me like they need me. I deal with a lot of pain, but when I'm on horseback, I do not feel that pain. It's the only thing that works. I have to take a lot of pain pills, but I still get breakthrough pains. The only time I don't is when I'm riding."

Another thing I love about Lara is that she says what needs to be said with or without prompting. Without further questions from me, Lara continues, "We're all going to get knocked around in this life, and some of us are luckier than others on what happens. I used to call this 'my stupid arm' because I can't control it and sometimes it does stuff that I hate. My friend said, 'Don't call that your *stupid* arm. That is your *lucky* arm. It saved your life. It took the brunt of that post — otherwise you would be in a wheelchair or you'd be dead.' I gave my right arm so I could live. It took me a few years to realize that. I had to get through the anger and mourning. Don't ever tell someone when they first get injured, 'It could be so much worse.' Or 'You should be thankful.' If they come to that conclusion, they need to do it on their own."

Lara's story is a compelling one for me, because it focuses on her abilities, not her "disabilities." When I first met her, I briefly felt pity for her; it didn't take Lara long to show me that she could do everything I could do as well as I could do it — and sometimes even better. She reminds me of Hester from *The Scarlet Letter;* by the end of the book, the scarlet letter on Hester's breast didn't stand for "adultery" anymore, it stood for "able." To me, Lara is the very embodiment of "able."

I was raised to believe that my body was a gift, that it was special and I needed to take care of it. We're constantly being bombarded by images of what the "perfect" body should be. On social media, there are articles about and exercise routines for getting the perfect arms, a flat stomach, a perky derriere, shapely legs, and let's not forget the all-important thigh gap. And yes, I'll admit, I've fallen prey to wanting to look a certain way, weigh a certain number, and getting completely caught up in how I look in not only jeans but in spandex — the love-hate relationship, looks versus comfort. In general, I feel good about the way I look, but there have been times when I haven't appreciated everything my body can do. It took being pregnant to open my eyes to how amazing my body really is.

I did not enjoy my first pregnancy at all. I'm not the nicest me that I can be when I'm pregnant, probably because I feel like I can't breathe or sleep and have to be in a thirty-second proximity to a bathroom at all times. Nor do I particularly enjoy the different comments from other people, like, "Oh, I see you've got a bun in the oven," or "I can see you're in the family way," or "You look like you're ready to pop." I understand the good intentions, but I find all these comments distasteful and obnoxious. And I admit, I said a few of these things before I was the pregnant lady on the receiving end of them. Now I don't.

During my pregnancy with Chloé, I worried — like any expectant parent — that I had this child growing inside me and yet I didn't feel any great love for the baby. All I could feel at the time was this alien taking over my body and preventing me from doing anything fun or enjoying a single night's rest without having to get up and go to the bathroom twenty times. *What's wrong with me?* I wondered. I worried about what would happen if she came out and I still didn't feel all those fluffy domestic feelings a mommy is *supposed to* feel.

And then I was in the hospital. Labor had begun. Matthew was there with me, holding my hand. At one point I remember being in so much pain, I wanted to ask the doctor to make it stop. I wasn't ready yet! But then I realized: There's only one direction for this baby to go, and it's not backwards. When Chloé emerged, perfect and beautiful and, yes, covered in blood, I remember crying, not tears of pain any longer but tears of pure emotion. She was beautiful. And she was mine. I had created her. My body had created her. I remember holding her in my arms for the first time right after she was born, her little body next to mine, knowing that there was nothing more precious or beautiful in the whole world, knowing that from that day forward, I would do anything for her, to keep her safe, to keep her healthy, to keep her happy, and to make sure she always knows how much she is loved.

As I recovered, I was in awe at what my body had done, the hard work it had put into creating this little person without any conscious effort from me. I started to love my body more than ever before — never mind the flabby stomach, breasts three times their normal size, and crazy spontaneous hormone sweats that would happen as my body readjusted to not having a baby inside.

I look at my daughter now, and I don't want her to worry about a number on the scale. I don't want her to see supermodels or Photoshopped women and try to attain in real life what can actually be attained only by a skilled artist on a computer screen. I hope she realizes that our bodies are gifts, that they are the one-of-a-kind, very special vessels that hold our spirits while we walk through this earthly life. I love that old saying "We're not physical beings having a spiritual experience; we're spiritual beings having a physical experience." But that physical experience does have a profound effect on our spirit. That's what I want my daughter to keep in mind when she sees her body in the mirror so that she respects that body and takes care of it and loves it.

While I was pregnant, I took my health very seriously. I wanted to make sure I remained healthy throughout pregnancy and afterward. I reached out to Helen Golden, a trainer at the gym I go to. She suggested we meet in person first to decide if we got along, to see if we were a good match as trainer and client. I had never had a professional trainer suggest that to me before. It was usually just "Yes, I have an opening" or "No, I don't have an opening." It hadn't really occurred to me before that a personal trainer is just as much about the personal as they are about the training. I was excited and, for some strange reason, nervous about meeting her. I'm a pretty easygoing person. I may not always agree with everyone, but I don't become explosive or bullheaded when someone disagrees with me or suggests a different point of view. But this was a blind date of sorts, and I really wanted her to like me.

I had no reason to be nervous. Helen is kind, all about the motivation, but very human and grounded at the same time. She started training me the following week, and she's been training me ever since. After I had Chloé, I told her, "I want to be physically stronger and have a greater endurance. I really hope that Chloé never worries about body image, but if she ever does, I hope she'll know what she needs to do to change because she sees me taking care of my body and exercising."

I had been what you might call an on-again-off-again runner, good one month, bad the next. Helen suggested that I try running a half marathon: 13.1 miles. At first I laughed out loud. I live a pretty active life, horseback riding almost year-round, skiing in the winter, and I have two dogs with lots of energy, but I felt like running three miles was a half marathon for me. Still, I thought about what Helen said and ultimately decided to give it a shot. I decided to run the Thankful 13 Thanksgiving half marathon. I ended up recruiting my older brother, my sister, her husband, her sister in-law, and my friend and running buddy to take on the challenge as well. It helped me so much, not just having people to run it with but having to be accountable to them. Every time Helen and I met, she asked if I had been completing my runs, stretching, and paying attention to nutrition. I wasn't perfect, but pretty soon I was running eight and nine miles without stopping.

Thanksgiving finally came, and I was up bright and early at the starting line. I did not look glamorous at all. I had on a black fluffy hat, a bright blue pullover, fuzzy gray gloves, black spandex pants, and my bright-green running shoes that look like I stole them from the circus. My sister showed up looking like a movie star, her whole outfit coordinated and sleek — no fuzzy anything — not to mention her beautiful eyelash extensions, which she doesn't even need because her eyelashes are just plain ridiculous to begin with, and her hair in a high ponytail with a sporty little ear band. Another important lesson for my daughter: Never compare yourself to other women. Down that road lies despair.

The half marathon ended up being a lot of fun. It was really hard, but I was so happy I did it. I'm pretty sure I came in 523rd out of over 900, and no, that's not exactly what you would call competitive, but I was so proud of myself just for doing it — and for completing it without walking once. I was also secretly happy that I beat my flawless, gorgeous sister by a couple minutes. The rest of the day, my legs felt like Jell-O, and I avoided moving as much as possible, but if anything gives you the green light to eat whatever and however much you want on Thanksgiving, running a half marathon does.

I couldn't wait to report my success back to Helen, who has been a contender in the fitness world for many years, and who was thrilled for me — which isn't to say she was ready to go easy on me. She consistently challenged me and pushed me. It got me thinking about the connection of total personal well-being and physical fitness, and I asked her if she'd come by my house and talk with me about that one day after she was done training her other clients.

She knocks on my door just as I'm putting away the vacuum. I'm constantly waging war with my floor because of the quantity of white dog hair that appears almost as quickly as I can clean it up. I invite her in, and we both make ourselves comfortable on the sofa in my family room. I dive right in with the big question: "How has staying in shape helped you through emotional or trying times in your life?"

"There is one incident that I remember and fall back to with my own clients," says Helen. "I tell them you have to be strong enough to push or pull your own body weight, because you never know when someone is going to need your strength. I remember very vividly being in an auto accident with an eighteen-wheeler with both my babies in the backseat. It was very scary. The car was totaled. But being as physically capable as I was at that time in my life, I was able to get out of the car and get both of my babies out of the backseat and comfort them. You never know when you might need to be there for somebody else."

Helen's hierarchy of priorities is just like mine: Family is more important than anything, but I believe in that airplane safety lecture philosophy of parenting that says you have to put your own oxygen mask on first or you won't be able to help anyone else.

"There is a definite connection between the mind, body, and spirit," she says. "They're all feeding each other, and when you have an unhealthy physical body, things are not functioning at an optimum, therefore your brain is not thinking at its highest potential, and your spirit would then be running at a much lower level. It's all connected."

That does make perfect sense to me. Too many times I've sacrificed sleep for work or not taken the time to prepare a healthy meal, opting instead for something quick and easy, and I always regret it later, feeling the sleep deprivation or the bloating and heavy feeling of indigestible food in my stomach distracting me from completing the task at hand. This is a problem that frequently confronts college students. We accept too easily that a student's life automatically means late nights, early mornings, vending-machine food — not a good combination.

In Helen's world, fitness is a combination of four basic components: "First, there's cardio. I love running because I get the endorphins with that. Second, there's lifting. I love weight lifting because it makes me feel so empowered and strong as a woman. Third, there's stretching, which is Pilates for me. I love Pilates because it's such a mental game, one of the highest forms of connecting the brain to the body. I love that challenge, and it's an ongoing challenge. I'm never too confident to say I've mastered it because I don't think you *can* master it. You just continue to fine-tune it. Fourth, there's balance. Working on balance is a great way to rehab when you're injured, plus now that I'm getting older balance is becoming more important."

"Do you think taking care of your body and staying fit helps you recover more quickly?"

Helen pauses for a moment, thinking, and then says, "That's actually a double-edged sword. I'm so active, I'm prone to injury. As a matter of fact, I have osteoarthritis because of overuse of my body. But compared to other women my age with that condition, I'm able to outperform them because of my lifestyle. So ultimately, yes, I do recover quicker, and I'm able to perform at a higher level than most women my age."

Thinking about my awesome half marathon, I know I was more consistent and determined because I had a goal set for myself, but I wonder if everyone is like that

— and if it's like that from the other side of the personal trainer equation. I ask Helen, "When you train, do you do it better when you're working toward a goal?"

"Absolutely," she says, nodding. "And when I'm working for a goal of my own — say, a running event — I'll intentionally pick a route where I know there's going to be a lot of traffic, because there's always the case of running into someone who knows me. If I'm not performing at the level they expect, then I'm just slacking off, and I can't have that. Having a goal gives me something to work for."

Helen is highly disciplined, and I admire that. I'm a sucker for freezer burritos, late-night pizza, and those waxy chocolate Donettes made by Hostess. What can I say? I'm a work in progress. But I have come a long way. Now the chocolate Donettes are only an occasional treat, and I have not had a freezer burrito since the last time they were passing them out as samples at Costco. Helen has helped me set the bar higher for myself physically than it ever has been before. Things that I thought I couldn't do before — like my half marathon — I realize I can do now. I need to train for them, but they are within my ability to accomplish.

I ask Helen, "Have you ever struggled?" I

know this sounds blasé and a bit silly coming from me, but she is so strong, physically and emotionally, I can't imagine her struggling with anything within her power to control.

She pauses for a minute, like she wants to say something but is taking time to consider whether it's really a good idea to share. And then she takes a deep breath and says, "Well, when I was in college . . . a freshman in a military junior college . . . I was raped. Rumors then flew around campus that I was promiscuous. Word got all the way up to the administrative staff, and I was very ashamed and embarrassed and didn't know how to deal with it, so I talked to my father, who was an army officer. I asked him, 'What should I do?' "

She doesn't tell me how he responded, but what she says next makes it clear.

"Back then sexual harassment was swept under the rug, so I felt very alone. It has affected me on a very personal basis, in my relationships, where the visual or the memories would come to me, and I'd just have to take a deep breath. I've dealt with it, and I've been honest with my husband about those things. That's how we've been able to continue to have a strong marriage. He knows when I need a shoulder to lean on.

But if you don't deal with it, and talk about it, and acknowledge it, then it can own you. And I don't want to be owned by that. Not at all."

One insidious side effect of sexual abuse for many survivors is damage to that sense of ownership. So many of the rape survivors I've met with are visibly uncomfortable in their own bodies, hiding inside baggy clothes or fighting back in self-destructive ways. It's hard for them to rebuild a healthy mind and spirit, because their body has become this unwelcoming environment. And it's sometimes hard to rebuild their bodies, because they've been told — by words and/or actions — that their body has no value. Reclaiming that value, cherishing that body they live in, might be the first step toward recovery, but it can also be one of the most difficult.

Whoever you are, whatever your shape, size, or level of fitness, I promise you, your body is amazing. It's beautiful. Our bodies are worth cherishing and caring for and defending just as fiercely as we do our homes, cars, clothes — whatever it is that we value.

I love that Lara now calls her arm her "lucky" arm because of the wisdom of a friend pointing out to her that she would be dead or a quadriplegic right now if her arm had not sacrificed itself for her. And I love that Helen, after her body was violated in one of the most devastating ways possible, fought back by loving herself. She recognized that if she didn't take the proper steps, that experience would own her. The ability to physically heal is intricately interwoven with emotional and psychological healing. It's really pretty miraculous how our bodies have the ability to mend bones and overcome illness, to respond to our commands, and to create life.

So why is it, do you suppose, that we're so harshly judgmental of our bodies?

Why do we "treat" ourselves with things that are actually self-destructive?

And how do we make it easier for our children — especially our daughters — to love and cherish these beautiful, powerful, amazing bodies they've been born with?

8
Building a Life of Love

My life has been a tapestry of rich and royal hue . . .
> — Carole King, "Tapestry"

We are all hurt one way or another, and it is love that heals. I think "finding support" means building supportive relationships. Because at the end of the day, relationships are what life is all about. Finding the important, uplifting, healthy ones makes all the difference in who we are and the choices we make, and sometimes we find them in unexpected ways. The more we allow our love out into the world, the more we see the common ground. I am constantly seeing this pattern of love over and over again, across all trials and walks of life.

"For me, my life was church, school, and home," says human rights activist Angeline Jackson. "I was a homebody. I was a church girl." This is common ground we share. Our stories are thousands of miles apart but parallel in many ways. Like me, Angeline accepted herself, loved her family, served her community, and reached out into the world. Like mine, her path was interrupted, but she found it again.

Angeline grew up in a tight-knit Christian family in Jamaica, the daughter of a pastor and a Sunday school superintendent, knowing from a young age that she is a lesbian. She began volunteering with her parish's AIDS Association while she was in high school, providing support to young people and families affected by HIV, which brought her into contact with people in the LGBT community. When Angeline was nineteen, she agreed to meet a troubled young woman who'd contacted her online, asking for help. Wanting to be cautious about meeting a stranger in a bad neighborhood, Angeline asked a friend to go with her. As the two girls walked to the place where the meeting was supposed to take place, two men approached them. One of the men said he was the stepbrother of the woman Angeline had been talking with online. In fact, the woman was part of a plan to "cure" Angeline and her friend of their homosexuality. Angeline's friend was brutally raped by both men. When they discovered Angeline was on her period, they forced her to her knees and orally raped her with a gun to her head.

"We were targeted and raped, my friend and I, just for being lesbians," says Angeline. "It was at gunpoint, and that was a moment of seeing my life flash before my eyes."

This wasn't an isolated incident. Angeline tells me she's heard similar stories from four other LGBT women who were lured into the same trap by someone pretending to need help. Sitting in my kitchen with my phone to my ear, I try to process one woman's inconceivable betrayal of another.

"How did you move forward from such a horrible experience?" I ask. "You were so young. Could you even process what had happened?"

"That resulted in a period of just trying to identify what it is that I needed to do. At nineteen, I asked myself a question: What have I done to contribute to society? If I were to die now, could I say that I have done anything for someone else? I processed that question in the months after the attack, realizing there wasn't really anything I could say. I recognized — as a lesbian and somebody who had experience sexual violence — there wasn't anywhere to go if something like this happened. Who did we turn to? Who did we go to?"

It took time for Angeline to work through the physical and emotional impact of the attack. More than anything, she was heartsick that she'd asked her friend to come with her. But in the seven years since that terrible night, Angeline has found her way back to herself and continued her efforts to reach out and help others. She went back to volunteering with the HIV/AIDS community and had the opportunity to go to the 2012 World AIDS Conference in Washington, D.C., which is where she heard the term "quality of citizenship for all people" in a meeting with the World Bank.

"I was very excited about that term," says Angeline, "because for me, that covered everything. It wasn't specifically sexual, it wasn't specifically LGBT."

Still in her early twenties, she cofounded a nonprofit organization called Quality of Citizenship Jamaica, which works with and supports lesbian, bisexual, and trans persons in her community.

I'll be totally honest here and say that of all the interviews I pursued as I gathered the stories I wanted to share in this book, this conversation with Angeline is the one I've been most nervous about. Because I was raised to view homosexuality from a conservative Christian point of view, I'm worried that I'll say something politically incorrect or ask a question in a way that comes off as disrespectful or unkind. And this is piled on top of the sensitivity required when discussing any experience of sexual assault. I have personally been on the receiving end of questions that are less than thought out, questions that may not come from a cruel intention but are nonetheless blunt, unfeeling, and insensitive. I often find myself inwardly bristling at these questions. Usually, the first things that come to mind are some stinging comebacks, but thank goodness, my brain usually intercedes before my tongue lashes back. Most people don't mean to be insensitive; they're just genuinely curious and don't know how to ask, so they say the first thing that comes to mind.

As the pause on the telephone lengthens, I struggle not to treat Angeline in the manner I so often find distasteful. How do I ask a question without being tactless? How do I not sound like a racist, homophobic jerk? The harder I try, the more I feel myself stumbling all over the place, trying to find the right wording, and while my mind races, the silence on the line is passing from that acceptable pause phase to the awkward pause phase where almost anything out of my mouth next is going to sound lame. I take a breath and return to that common ground we share. The homebody. The church kid.

"What was your childhood like?"

"I grew up in a very service-oriented family," she says. "I didn't even process that until I just said it. I just grew up doing service. I was baptized in the church at a very early age, and with that came the responsibility of ministry and doing outreach. That was where my foundation was built. I would go out and do tract distribution with different groups in different neighborhoods around the city."

"In high school, when you volunteered with the parish AIDS Association, did your parents know?"

"They knew about it," says Angeline. "I think the reason they didn't react negatively was that my mom also taught at that school, so she knew the teacher who headed the association. My parents didn't know that, for me, that was a space in which I could find LGBT people. It was about a space in which I could help others, and that was how I told them about it. Volunteering opened my eyes to so much I hadn't known because of growing up in the country. Having a strict Christian family, things like sexuality and sexual health were not discussed. While volunteering, I was able to learn and then impart my knowledge to other young people. I was happy just being around gay people. The volunteer work was a combination of different things, but all helped me figure out who I was."

"I imagine it was very difficult when you told your parents —" I stop myself, not sure if I'm overstepping. "If you don't want to answer this question — I mean, I want to be completely respectful of you. I don't want you to feel like I'm — If I ever go too far, please just say you don't feel comfortable telling me. It's just . . . I'm curious about the conflict between how you were raised and who you are now. How did your family react when you came out?"

"There is a complicated answer to a very simple question," says Angeline, "because the first time I told my parents anything was when I was thirteen. I was still at St. Hilda's High, which was the all-girls school, and there were rumors going around church that I liked girls. I wanted to make sure that I was the person who told my mother. I did not want it to come from anybody else. While I was not ready to come out, I already knew how I felt, but I told Mommy just in the matter of saying it to her before she heard through the grapevine at church. Mommy's reaction was to pray for me. She prayed, and that was the end of that discussion."

When Angeline was sixteen, people were threatening to beat her up at school, so her parents moved her to a different high school and sent her to "ex-gay therapy."

"The purpose of that," she says, "was to identify the root cause for why I liked girls and to help me develop a liking for boys, but I stopped very early with that. I told my parents, 'We're wasting your money, and we're wasting my time, and I'm not going back.'"

"Good for you."

"Sometimes in hindsight when I think about all the things I did between thirteen and sixteen, I was really stupid, because it could have gone really wrong. Really badly. But it didn't. Later on, in my twenties, at one point, I was very low emotionally. I was self-harming, and my doctor had given me Valium, and since I was pumped up on medication, completely devoid of emotion, I decided to go home and speak with them. I thought, *I've never told my parents the whole story. I can't judge them, because I haven't given them the chance.* I'm very happy I did it at that point. I was very open with them. At the end of the conversation, my parents said, 'We love you as our daughter, but the Bible says that homosexuality is a sin.' "

"Do you still have a relationship with your parents?"

"I still do. Outside of my being gay, we have a very good relationship. We just don't talk about it."

"Is that hard for you?"

"It is. It's very hard, because within the context of Jamaica, and a population of three million, I'm not just a regular everyday gay person. I'm very well known in the LGBT community in Jamaica. I'm very well known among people who are really *anti-*gay in Jamaica. When President Obama was in Jamaica and mentioned me as a young leader, I know my parents were happy, but it was this conflicted happiness of 'We're happy for you, but we can't be fully happy, because the reason you were mentioned is because you're gay, and because you're very public about being gay.' It's complicated."

"Having gone through everything that you have gone through, there must be times when you feel alone or hurt or lost. Where do you turn to for peace?"

"In 2009 I wasn't going to church, and I found this online community, the Gay

Christian Network. I very much relied on that community in the days and months after the rape. I got a lot more in touch with my faith during that period. That was probably the most Christian or spiritual I've ever been. I relied heavily on faith, and I listened to a lot of gospel songs. About a year or two afterwards, I had done a course on reconciling the Bible and homosexuality. It was not something I needed to do for myself personally, but it was something I wanted to do so that I would have the knowledge to be able to respond to my dad or some other religious person who tried to pick an argument with me. After that, I went through a period of agnosticism. I really didn't rely on much of anything at that time. I've never been a person to cope very well with downtime, and especially at that moment, I made sure to be very, very active, very involved with school, involved in volunteer work, just very invested in anything else that made sure that I did not have downtime. I was on a panel at Founders Metropolitan Community Church in Los Angeles, and let's put it this way: I don't think God uses relationships to get people back to God, but in this case, I think there was an exception to that rule, because that's where I met my partner. That was my first time dating somebody who was exactly my age. Somebody who wanted to be a pastor. I had never heard that from anybody before. A lesbian who wanted to be a pastor! It was there, with her, that communication. I really started to get back in that space of spirituality."

That space, I realize, is the true common ground Angeline and I share. I know how it feels to be torn apart, lost, and confused — at some point or another most of us do. Difficult times befall us all, and unfortunately, they don't disappear immediately. While we're going through difficulties and challenges, it's not uncommon to lose ourselves. And it may sound too simple to be true, but I think love for others is how we find ourselves again. When we start giving back to society, serving others, and doing good deeds and acts of kindness, we are changed during the process. We find our better selves through love for those around us, a love of reaching out and working for a cause throughout humanity.

It's easier said than done. The pitfalls along this path include overwhelming grief and anger we are unable to accept, feel, and then let go. Shutting ourselves off from the world and those who love us seems like a sturdy self-defense mechanism, because sometimes the people close to us have the leverage to hurt us the most.

Shortly after I was rescued, because of the massive amount of publicity surrounding my story, there were many people scrambling to write books and make movies about what had happened to me — and these things were happening without my approval. As a fifteen-year-old who just desperately wanted to get back to a normal life, I became very angry. How dare anyone try to write about something they didn't have the slightest clue about? What right did they have to say anything about this horrible, humiliating thing that had been done to me — much less cash in on it? And worst of all, one of the many people threatening to come out with a publication was my uncle. I was very hurt and felt betrayed. This wasn't an uncle who was far away and unknown to me. He was someone I'd gone horseback riding with many times, someone I admired and wanted to be like. He seemed to know everyone and had done so much, always going on adventures for work or with his family, an absolute cowboy up in the saddle, and more important, I had always considered him a friend. How could this be fair? I had just lost nine months of my life, and then I came back only to feel betrayed by my own family.

Despite my objections and my parent's objections, he went ahead with the project. He published a book about what had happened, even though I had begged him not to. I did receive a copy of his book, and as I started reading it, I became angrier and angrier. I finally ripped up parts of the book, because I couldn't stand what had been written. I'm not a violent person, and I had never ripped apart a book before and haven't since, but I couldn't stand it. Unfortunately, the real damage that this book caused was within the family. My family became divided. Some of my aunts and uncles sided with us; some did not. We went about a year avoiding family get-togethers and speaking to each other as little as possible. That was tragic, because I always thought that what made my family so special and unique was how much we all cared about each other and how close we stayed, supporting each other no matter what. It seemed as if all of that had been destroyed almost instantly.

My dad was the one who, for my side of the family, bridged the gap. He took me aside and told me that no matter what had happened, he still loved everyone; he was hurt by what they had done, but they were still his brothers and sisters.

"If something were to happen tomorrow or next year," he said, "I don't want to be the one wishing I had made amends."

I realized he was right. I missed my family. My love for them was bigger than my anger and disappointment. We started coming back to family parties and reunions. I was surprised at how easy it was to forget about everything with everyone — well, almost everyone. Everyone except my one uncle. I was still harboring some harsh feelings toward him. But at the end of the next summer, I finally found myself alone with my uncle at my grandparents' ranch. I decided I should take the opportunity to express my feelings and unburden myself of the negative baggage I'd been carrying around because of him. I took my chance, and it was not easy. I'm not a very confrontational person, even if I feel I'm in the right. But I found the strength to speak up for myself. I told him how he had hurt me and asked him how he could have done that. He has three daughters of his own and would not hesitate to rip into anyone who hurt them, yet he could do what he did to me? Tears began running down his face. He apologized and offered to give me the money, but I wanted nothing to do with that. It was too late to undo what had been done. There was nothing else he could do but ask for my forgiveness.

I knew I was at a crossroads. I had to make a decision: continue on and let all of this go, or hold on to my anger at his betrayal, the repulsive words I had read, and the cover of the book, which still conjures images of shredded paper in my mind. I knew which choice was the right one to make, but it was hard. I told him I was speaking to him because I was forgiving him, but I wanted him to know how much he had hurt me, and I made it clear that our relationship wasn't just going to go back to what it once was.

That was over a decade ago. My uncle and I have moved on since that point. We still go horseback riding together and chat at family get-togethers. The past is not spoken of anymore, and I don't dwell on it. I am so grateful for a dad who isn't afraid to show his daughter what it means to forgive someone you love and still love them. I value and love my uncle. And it has been through love that our relationship was healed.

It crosses my mind to share this story with Angeline. It feels a bit like another acre of common ground. But this is about her, so I ask, "When you look back on it all — on the people who've hurt you — do you ever struggle with grief or anger?"

"Grief, not anger. I've definitely felt anger. Different instances have caused different measures of anger, but I've definitely felt grief in the sense of sexual violence. I felt grief for myself, but I felt more grief and guilt regarding my friend, who has never spoken out, who has never sought medical resources for what she experienced — somebody who came to give me support. I feel very guilty about what she experienced. I've had to just be present and be a friend, continuously checking in, finding out how she's doing, calling. That's what I've been able to do while learning to not have guilt about what had happened."

"And what about your family?"

"I definitely have had grief as it related to my family and my family's difficulty in accepting me. It's an anticipatory grief right now. How are they going to respond when I introduce them to the person who is in my life? What are they going to do when I get married? What are they going to do when I have kids? At the same time, I think there is hope, so where the grief is very present, I'm still young enough that I will say, 'Hold on to that hope.' I think especially with gay people, hope is what we all do. We hope that, at some point, the people who mean the most to us will be able to accept, to understand, and to love us."

"Have you forgiven the people who've hurt you in your life? And if so, how?"

"Wow," Angeline says. "I never even considered that question. Being able to see other stories and learn why people do some of the things they do — as silly or as stupid as they might seem from my end — I'm able to sometimes look from the perspective of the other person. That has made it more likely to be able to forgive. I've forgiven the stepbrother. I've forgiven the man who had the gun. I've forgiven the woman. How, I don't know."

I don't know either. In fact, I find it shocking when Angeline says she has forgiven the woman who set up the rape. That part of the story is almost worse for me than the actual rape, knowing that a fellow woman targeted Angeline and her friend — two people who were willing to go down a dark street in order to help her, only to be raped just because this woman didn't agree with their sexual orientation. There is never any excuse that could possibly make rape the right thing to do. It doesn't matter what you believe, your political views, your personal standards, or your religion — nothing could ever give one person the right to sexually violate another person. I'm still upset by Angeline's story.

"I can't believe it was a woman who set it up," I tell her. "That makes me so angry."

Angeline calmly responds, "I have in some ways moved past the situation, but I don't 100 percent forgive her. She messaged me just the other day, asking for my phone number to speak with me, and I said, 'You know what? Let's just keep our conversation here on Facebook, because in all honesty, I don't want to give you my number.' I really do not know how I have managed that forgiveness, because of all the different hurts, that is the biggest. At the same time, it's also been the catalyst for my change and who I have become. If I could repeat history — I don't know — people usually say, 'If you could go back, would you change this?' I don't know, because then I wouldn't be who I am. I wouldn't have had the experiences I've had. I wouldn't have my partner. But for the sake of my friend who was raped, I would give anything to change that."

I hear the pain in her voice, and I do understand where it's coming from, but it seems to me that the guilt that haunts her is one more thing her attackers had no right to inflict on her.

"I think my forgiveness . . . it came after time," Angeline says. "It's been almost ten years since it happened. It's been a process of getting to the point of forgiveness, but my forgiveness has come with being able to turn something horrific into something I could triumph over, something I could stand on, and something that has made me a better person. It definitely has been the catalyst for me to become who I am. I think that is why I have been able to forgive."

I ask her again, "What about your family?"

"I've forgiven my parents, and that was very recent. I was at a support group meeting in California, and someone said that we need to consider that at the time we came out, we had X number of years to come to the recognition and the realization that we are gay. Our parents are only just getting started with the process of being able to accept that. For me, that made sense. It hurts, and I would very much like them to one day get to the point of being able to fully accept me. For now, I'll give them — let's say sixteen years. That's how long I had to work through coming out to myself."

I glance at the clock and see that we've gone over the time she agreed to give me, so I thank Angeline for her willingness to be open about all this, and I nudge her to answer one more question. "Before I let you go, what advice would you share with survivors of sexual violence — particularly anyone in the LGBT community who's been targeted or abused because of their sexual orientation?"

"I moved some time ago from being a victim to being a survivor, but survival is a daily process. For survivors of sexual violence, I think what I would say is, find that support, people who can rally around you, people who can hold you up when there is nothing under your feet, people who can hold you in moments like those, people who can support you and give you that strength. We find strength in many different places, and I think it's about identifying where that strength is. For some people, that strength is faith. For other people, faith is the problem. It's about identifying what works best for your healing yourself and not destroying you. I say that because for me, self-harm was a way of healing, because I was able to physically see my pain, but in doing that, I was still hurting myself. I drank because it was a way to dull the pain, but in drinking, it was damaging my body."

This sends a cold shiver down my spine, because my mind goes immediately to the darkest moments during my captivity. First, my captors forced alcohol on me so I'd be easier to control, but I learned quickly that the alcohol would make me oblivious for a little while, and oblivion was the only relief I had, so I forced the alcohol on myself, even though it left me vomiting and miserable.

"Who we are will be the great determining factor in what works best for our healing and for our surviving," says Angeline. "Recognizing that we want to live, always working towards the next day, one step at a time. Sometimes all that can be done is stepping one foot in front of the other. For me, each day is a matter of surviving, of living. What I would want somebody to know about me is that I'm a survivor, and we each have the capacity to survive and to thrive. I'm not yet thriving, but I'm on my way to thriving. Each of us has the capacity — whatever horrific incident we've ever faced in our lives — we have a capacity to survive and then thrive."

Taking in all that Angeline has accomplished in that ten years, not with a "gay agenda" but with the idea that all people are entitled to equal rights and protection from violence, an agenda that goes back to her Christian roots — "Love thy neighbor as thyself" — I realize that sometimes the trickiest part of that is starting with the "love thyself" part: to know and love yourself as you are, to accept and love your family as they are, to take that love out into your community, and empowered by the knowledge that there is something you can do for others, become what Jesus described as "the light of the world."

In the days following my rescue, I didn't want anyone to know what had happened to me, especially not any of the sexual abuse that I had endured. I remember sitting with my family one night in my parents' bedroom and seeing on the TV a sentence that kept repeating itself at the bottom of the screen: "Elizabeth Smart is not pregnant." I was horrified that anyone could even have thought I might be. Beyond the fact that I didn't want people to know that could have even been a possibility, I just wanted everyone to leave what had happened to me alone and pretend that I was the same as any other young woman. I felt that all the sexual abuse and violence had somehow set me apart and made me different, and I just wanted to be the same as everyone else.

My parents were very sensitive to how I felt at the time and did all they could to protect me and help me to feel normal. As the years passed and I grew and matured, I began to meet other survivors of sexual violence and abuse, and despite knowing the statistics of how common rape is, I was still dumbfounded every time I had another face to connect with that statistic. After I returned home from serving my LDS mission in Paris, I asked my dad what he thought I could do that would help make a difference, that would be worthwhile. He looked at me and said, "Elizabeth, one thing that you could do is share your story. Try public speaking. Share your story however you feel comfortable."

I think my initial reaction was a snort of laughter. Who on earth would listen to me share me story? I was not a public speaker. I had not ever sought the limelight nor enjoyed it when it was thrust upon me. But his words stayed in my head. Maybe I should try. I did after all testify during the trial, and wasn't it then that I decided that I wanted to write a book about my story? To set the record straight? And wasn't that another way of trying to help other victims and survivors? Why would speaking be so bad? Most of the sexual abuse came out when I was on the stand anyway; it wasn't a secret. People knew. It was a matter of public record now. By this time in my life, I had accepted what had happened to me and realized that there is never any turning around in life, there is only going forward. Fortunately, through the love of the best parents and family in the world, I was able to overcome the traumatic experience. I knew that what had happened to me didn't make me any less of a person. Despite all the lessons I'd heard growing up — about remaining pure and abstaining from sex until marriage — I knew that no one person could destroy what I was born with: value.

I decided to give public speaking a try. My first real speech was at a community college in Petoskey, Michigan. I was so nervous the whole flight from Salt Lake City to Detroit, and then from Detroit to the small regional airport in nearby Petoskey. There was someone from the college waiting to pick me up. As I got into the car, I was told there was great excitement about my arrival and forthcoming speech. I sat in the seat looking out the window. It was autumn, and the leaves were vibrant hues of red, orange, and yellow. Despite the beauty around me, I wished I were anywhere but there. I didn't know if I'd be good enough to do this. I'd prepared a binder probably three inches thick with notes. I kept reminding myself, *Tomorrow will still come and you will still be a good person.*

The moment finally arrived. I walked up onstage and started speaking. My voice was shaking from nerves, but I pushed on through to the end. I don't remember exactly what I said, but I remember the feeling I got from the audience: overwhelming understanding and gratitude. I remember their tears and the feeling that I truly had been able to make a small difference in their lives. The more speaking I did, the more comfortable I felt in front of a crowd. And then the most amazing thing started happening: Women started coming forward and saying that because of what I had shared, they were going to share what had happened to them. Sometimes it's overwhelming and exhausting — never more so than now, having to leave my little girl at home and being pregnant with baby number two — but I am still reminded of why I speak. Women may know that sex crimes happen, and they happen a lot, and it is completely normal to feel all of the negative feelings one can imagine. It's so important for victims to know that nothing can destroy their worth.

In the wake of a violent or traumatic experience, we're left to struggle with some of life's toughest questions: Will this thing that happened always define me, or will I redefine myself with the choices I make? Where will I find the strength to survive? And how will I find the strength to forgive?

9
THE POWER TO FORGIVE

> To forgive is to set a prisoner free and
> discover that the prisoner was you.
>
> — LOUIS B. SMEDES

I've talked about forgiveness in almost every
chapter of this book, because it's something
people ask about everywhere I go and it's a
thread that runs through every story I
heard: the struggle to either forgive the
people who harmed us or to forgive ourselves. Perhaps Martin Luther King Jr. said
it best: "We must develop and maintain the
capacity to forgive. He who is devoid of the
power to forgive is devoid of the power to
love. There is some good in the worst of us
and some evil in the best of us. When we
discover this, we are less prone to hate our
enemies."

The first time I heard about Chris Williams, I was sitting in church listening to a
lesson on forgiveness. The teacher turned

on a YouTube clip of a man who introduced himself and said, "I was born and raised in Salt Lake. I married Michelle Dorny, and we had four children together — Mike, Ben, Anna, Sam."

In the winter of 2007, Michelle was expecting their fifth child. The Williams family was on their way to get ice cream one evening when their car was struck by a seventeen-year-old boy who was driving drunk. Michelle was killed, along with the unborn baby, eleven-year old Ben, and nine-year-old Anna.

Only days after the accident that changed Chris Williams's family forever, there was a terrible shooting at a local mall. The shooter was a young man, practically a boy. Seven people died that day, and more were injured. At a press conference Chris had already scheduled in response to public outcry about the car accident, he spoke with genuine compassion for the young man who'd killed his wife and children. Then he asked the community to pray for the victims of the shooting, for the families who had lost their loved ones, and for the family of the young shooter, who had finally turned the gun on himself.

Chris's story stayed with me for a long time, partly because I just felt so heartbroken for him. My family has always been the one thing that I knew I could count on no matter what. Their being taken away is the worst thing I can think of. But beyond the heartbreak was Chris's astonishing response to it — and his call for compassion magnified his own ability to forgive. When I began this project, knowing I wanted to explore the complex topic of forgiveness, I immediately thought of Chris, who seemed so positive and peaceful. Everything I knew about him told me that he was one of the most extraordinary ordinary people I'd ever heard of.

When I reached out to Chris, he invited me to visit him at the home he now shares with his second wife, Mikkel, who lost her first husband to bone cancer. She had two children from her first marriage — Arli and Parker — and together, Chris and Mikkel have two daughters: Emma, born in 2009, and little Caroline, who was born in 2012, on Ben's birthday, coincidentally. "So that turned out to be a sweet experience," Chris said. We agreed to meet the following week, and when he shared his new address with me, it rang a bell.

Now I know why. As I follow the GPS instructions around the corner, I realize that Chris lives just a couple of houses down from my grandma and just around the corner from my aunts. It's a small world, after all. The neighborhood is pleasantly familiar: the bikes and toys scattered in front yards, the well-manicured lawns, and of course my grandma's redbrick house. It's a comforting feeling. This is going to be one of the more difficult interviews I've assigned myself, with a lot of hard questions. When I think of Chris's lost children, I get a lump in my throat.

I pull up and approach the front door and ring the bell. A young boy answers, and I ask, "Is your dad home?"

Chris comes up the stairs and invites me into their front living room. From the moment I walk into their home, I feel a certain peace, and I just know that this is a special family. Looking around the living room, I see a beautiful statue on a wooden buffet chest: a young mother with a small boy on one side, a little girl on the other, and a tiny baby in her arms. *The family he lost,* I think, and I immediately want to ask about it, but I feel it's hardly appropriate to do so before the usual niceties are shared.

Chris asks me about my project. What are my hopes for it? How did I think of it? Am I experiencing any difficulties getting people to commit? I tell him how grateful I am for the generosity and openness I've seen from people I've spoken with, though I'm trying to be sensitive in the way I ask the hard questions.

He understands and says, "You're free to ask whatever you like."

"Tell me more about the family you had with Michelle. What roles did the children play before the accident?"

Chris smiles as he remembers them. "Michael was a little bit more serious. Being the firstborn, he got a lot of the initial attention, but he was very active in sports. He was the athlete, did a lot of snowboarding, skateboarding, and played basketball. Ben was definitely the funniest of all. He just lived large. He was tremendously fun to be around and was certainly beyond his years in maturity. Anna was just sweet, probably the biggest peacemaker in the house. She was filled with love and had that feminine touch of wanting to wrap things in blankets and loving her dolls and animals. She wanted to be a veterinarian when she grew up. Then there was Sam, who is just all around fun. Soccer is his big thing now, but he grew up loving Thomas the Tank Engine. He used to sit and play with those for hours."

"What did your marriage to Michelle

mean to you?"

"It meant everything to me," Chris says. "Our relationship was just continually growing together and loving together. As I grew and developed as a person, her impact on me influenced that development, and what a positive impact that was. I married above myself. Some people will just roll their eyes when I say that. They'll just think, *Oh, okay, yeah, that sounds like a nice thing to say,* but for me, it was really, really true. She was just a superior person and helped me want to be a better person as well."

I take a big breath, thinking my words will come out faster if I don't have to stop for air. "What happened the day of the crash? Did you have any premonition of something bad coming?"

"No. Actually, it was the opposite. It was a phenomenal evening. In fact, looking back, it's interesting to see how the year prior to this was so amazingly perfect. The family trips we took together — we ended up taking a lot more trips than we usually did. My wife and I had the chance to take a couple's trip. Had an outstanding, amazing time. It left me and left our family with some incredibly sweet memories. It was a tender mercy that we had the time together."

"What happened that evening?"

Chris describes "just another Friday night" — a seemingly average evening in the life of a seemingly average family. "Michael had gone off with friends to a basketball game. Sam was off playing at a friend's house. At about seven, I said, 'Hey, let's go get Mexican food,' but Anna was watching a show on Animal Planet, sitting close to Michelle, and I was struck by how wonderful they looked. It's hard to explain, but I just had this moment where I absolutely appreciated how blessed we were. So instead of getting irritated, like, 'C'mon, let's go. I'm hungry,' it was more like, 'Okay, we'll wait.' "

After Anna's program, Chris and Michelle took Ben and Anna to a nearby Mexican restaurant, where they ran into some friends.

"Ben was cracking the funniest jokes," Chris says. "Everyone was happy. The memory of what I felt that night definitely helped me get through the tragedy and the separation from them. Just reminding myself that I did have it all. And I still do."

It was almost ten when they left the restaurant and picked up Sam from his friend's house, but the kids wanted to get ice cream cones at McDonald's, and Chris figured, *Why not?* That's what set them on the path to go underneath the 20th East underpass. Just going to get ice cream cones. I know exactly where that intersection is. I've driven through it many times myself. When I was little, we visited my grandma in that area, and my mom used to call that underpass the "bunny hole" because of the steep decline under the freeway and sudden incline on the other side. For a brief moment, right when you're about to go under the freeway, your view of oncoming traffic is obstructed. The speed limit there is 30 MPH. Police reports estimate that seventeen-year-old Cameron White was doing about 75.

"I saw headlights coming at us," says Chris. "It was so surreal. Just seeing the lights and no car behind it. My mind didn't process it immediately. It didn't make sense. Instead of realizing that we were going to be hit and that we were in danger, my mind was thinking, *What's going on? How should I react?* I did try to do something to avoid being hit, but it didn't matter."

Cameron swerved, struggling to correct his course, and struck the passenger side of the Williams family's car. According to police, even if Chris had gone left or right in that split second, he couldn't have avoided the catastrophic impact.

There are so many difficult questions to ask. For both our sakes, I want to get through this part. "What happened then? Or did it happen so quickly that . . . ?"

Chris pauses for a moment and looks very thoughtful. "I remember the sound. And I remember being hit so hard that it knocked my vision out. All I could see — all I could perceive — was white, and then as my vision slowly started to come back, I could see the glass from the imploded windshield still falling. Things just popped. Vaporized. I had an immediate sense of pain all over. I was shocked to still be alive after being hit so hard. I didn't know if Michelle was dead or alive at that moment. I finally got my hand over to hers and felt for a pulse. That's when I noticed that on her other elbow — the right elbow — she had a significant wound that was not bleeding. I had worked as an EMT for several years when I was younger and knew that when the heart was pumping with that kind of wound, there should be lots of bleeding. I checked for the pulse. I was desperately searching. I couldn't find one."

"Were you able to see your children in the backseat?"

"Initially, it was a struggle to even move.

When I was finally able to turn enough to see Ben, he had a significant gash on his head. It wasn't bleeding. Same thought. I wasn't able to touch him or feel for a pulse, but knowing that kind of head trauma and no blood and no sign of movement — that was not good. When I looked at Anna, her hair was covering her face. No movement at all. I couldn't see Sam, who was sitting directly behind me. I couldn't hear anything."

Chris was told later that Michelle, Ben, and Anna all died from "aortic separation": the force of the impact separating the heart from the carotid artery. We hear about tragedies of this magnitude on the news, and of course we feel heartbroken, we have compassion, but something about this detail makes it unbearably real. I feel it in my own bones. Tears brim in my eyes, but Chris is calm. No tears. I can't imagine how, but he seems to have truly come to peace with what happened. I wonder if perhaps he's spoken about it so much that it no longer feels like his life. There are times I feel that way, when I've been doing a lot of speaking about being kidnapped and raped. I don't become numb to it, but the magnitude of it all takes me outside of myself sometimes.

I move the story forward as gently as I

can. "So you knew then. That they were dead."

Chris nods. "After that realization, the grief hit. It was immediate, soul-compressing grief and anguish, quick and powerful — shocking how powerful it was. I felt like my life was done, and that's what I wanted. I remember putting my head against the window and trying to force my spirit out of my body. It was too much to be asked to see what I was seeing. It was almost out of body, because I heard a noise, and I didn't know where it was coming from, and then I realized it was coming from me. I was crying and wailing and making a horrible noise. In the midst of that, I saw the car that had just struck us. It was upside down, maybe fifty or a hundred feet up the road from us. When I saw the car, I quieted just enough to hear three words. *Let it go.* It felt so real — as if someone was speaking right over my shoulder. Like if I turned around, I would see someone there. Someone telling me, *Let it go.*"

The moment is so vivid, I can almost hear it myself. I ask Chris, "What did those words mean to you?"

"I felt it was specifically saying that I had to move forward with faith, not with anger or a desire for justice. I was going to do it the Lord's way, which would put me on a path of forgiveness, extension of mercy, relying on the Savior's grace. I needed to let go of my expectations that my wife and I would live our lives together into our nineties, let go of everything, my hopes and dreams. The only thing I was ever given was my ability to choose, to make decisions, and to let go of all other expectation or anticipation."

I understand all this, but I get stuck on the practical application, like tires spinning in powder snow: Let it go? How could you? Why would you? And why would a merciful God even ask that of anyone?

First responders used the "jaws of life" to extract Chris from the car, and as they were putting him into the ambulance, he heard Sam cry out. According to paramedics, as father and son were rushed to the hospital in critical condition, Chris kept saying, "We need to forgive the other driver." The first responders were astonished. They were fuming, sickened by what they were seeing, angry at the drunk driver. In the emergency room, Chris was told that the other driver was seventeen and had been drinking.

"I felt so broken," says Chris. "My lungs were filling up with water, so I felt like I was drowning. But I don't think my soul has ever felt so liberated. So free. Full of love. I knew the Savior was telling me, 'You know I love that boy as much as I love you and your family.' "

Maybe because I'm expecting, I can't help asking, "Did you ever see the baby?"

"At the funeral," he says. "First I closed the lid of Anna's casket, and then I closed the lid of Ben's casket, and then right before we closed Michelle's casket, they handed me this tiny baby. He looked so much like Sam, it was unbelievable. I took the baby and nestled him in my wife's arms, gave her a kiss, and closed the casket."

Looking away from Chris, trying to hide the tears running down my face, I see the statue again. "Is that your family?"

"Yes. Some friends got together after everything and had it made for me."

To me, it seems like the most significant thing in the room, a mother with her two children, cradling her baby in her arms. It's so beautiful, it makes me want to cry all the more. I swallow hard and go back to my list of questions. "Chris, do you ever feel anger toward Cameron, the young man who was driving drunk and hit you?"

"I definitely felt tons of anger. Tons of struggle. I haven't been spared any of the growing pains, so to speak. That's what happens when you're confronted with such a tragic kind of catastrophic change in your life and in your goals and plans and dreams and everything else, but through all of that, I think the one blessing that I have been given is that I've never directed my anger at Cameron."

I've listened to Chris's story many times, read his book, and listened to clips from speeches, but when he talks about Cameron, it always blows me away. There's no anger or malice; in fact, he shows the exact opposite: forgiveness and genuine concern. When I ask him if he feels the consequences faced by Cameron were just, Chris says, "I decided before the trial to let it go."

"Is that when you met Cameron?"

"We saw each other in court a couple months after the accident. We made eye contact, and he mouthed, 'I'm sorry,' but that was it."

The choice before the court was whether to try the seventeen-year-old as an adult. As an adult, Cameron could face thirty-five years in prison with hardened adult criminals. As a juvenile, he'd go to a juvenile detention center until age twenty-one, and then he'd be released with his record expunged.

"When I was on the stand," says Chris, "after all the evidence was shown and everything else, the judge asked me what I thought the penalty should be, and I told him, 'That's why you get paid the big bucks.' It made him laugh, but it was my way of saying, 'That's your job. I'm not going to answer that question.' I honestly did want what was best for Cameron. I didn't want him to become another tragedy, another victim of that night."

Cameron was tried as a juvenile, and about a year after the accident, Chris went to the detention facility to visit him. He told Cameron, "I bear you no ill will. We are brothers in this."

"Do you think that was a turning point for him?" I ask. "Meeting with you face-to-face?"

"Absolutely. When I first came into the room, it was just him and me and a counselor, and he had been lifting weights out there, so he was bulked up. He could have taken me easily. He was incredibly solemn, and his posture was very defensive. He had no idea. When I came in, I had a smile on my face and shook his hand, and I think it completely took him aback. He asked some prepared questions about how the crash had impacted my family and about my life going forward. The counselor said, 'Anything else you want to ask Mr. Williams?' And he just . . . the tears started to flow. He said, 'After everything I did to your family, how can you forgive me? How does somebody do that? How do you get there?' I told him that I was able to kind of bear witness. That for me, it was the grace of the Savior, that enabling power that helped me to do what I was doing, and he should know that he's got to do the same thing I did: pick a date and let it go. Just let it go, and move forward, and not let this define who he is."

"You told him to pick an actual date on the calendar and then to move on after that day?"

Chris nods, and again I feel tears in my eyes. No doubt that is easier said than done, but think how freeing that would be for this kid — for anyone who feels genuine remorse. It would be life-changing, I imagine.

I ask Chris, "Is that something that came to you in that moment? Or was that something you've practiced in your own life? I mean — I really think it's brilliant, actually."

"A lot of it was based on what I experienced. By that time, I'd had a year to reflect on it, a year to realize all of the blessings that personally have been coming because I made that choice. It didn't make it easier, didn't make the pain stop, but at least it gave me something to focus on. My path forward — that was my choice, so that's what I wanted him to do too. Have that *let it go* moment."

"Do you think he followed your advice?"

"Yes, absolutely. In fact, I had a chance to meet him in October of last year. I went to his wedding reception. He got released early, when he was twenty. He's absolutely made a decision. He has completely reinvented himself. He's been, I would say, almost reborn, which is wonderful. He's married now. Has a great home and a great job. He is a totally different person. That boy doesn't exist anymore."

Most of us are taught when we're small children that forgiveness happens when you apologize, and as small children, we most often have our parents standing right behind us, forcing us to mutter, "Sorry." Then as we grow into adults, it changes from that simple forced "sorry" into something else. I've thought and thought about how to describe it. I'm not sure I have the right words to articulate it. Sometimes it flies out of our mouths, second nature, and it's questionable whether or not we actually mean it.

So it's not unreasonable to be a little

skeptical when we're on the receiving end of an apology. The part of this dynamic I hadn't considered is the aspect Chris's story brings to light: the fact that the most difficult person to forgive is oneself. When we've been wronged, it's almost like the bigger or more traumatic the event has been, the more noble we look for forgiving, but when it comes to forgiving ourselves for wronging someone else — or wrongly feeling responsible for something terrible that's happened to us — it is almost impossible to let go. It's somehow easier to forgive strangers than to forgive ourselves or the people we know and love. There seems to be a spectrum — many levels and kinds of forgiveness — and quite honestly, it gets confusing.

I decide it would be a good idea to ask an expert, someone who hears confession and leads people through the act of atonement, and immediately archbishop John Wester of the Catholic Church comes to mind. I haven't actually met the archbishop yet, but I've been invited to speak at an event where he's going to be honored. The event planner who invited me has told me a lot about him, and everyone I've talked to about the event goes on for at least ten minutes singing his praises. So not long after my meeting with Chris, I call the archbishop, explain the basic idea of my quest, and ask if he has just a few minutes to talk. I quickly learn that Archbishop Wester seldom talks for just a few minutes, but I end up feeling deeply grateful for his thoughtful pauses and long, contemplative answers.

"What is forgiveness," I ask, "and how does it bring healing?"

He begins by repeating a wise saying that's been attributed in various forms to everyone from Confucius to Oprah: *Forgiveness is giving up hope of a better past.*

"Forgiveness is very important in healing," he goes on, "because forgiveness is not whitewashing, or pretending something didn't happen, or floating on the *Good Ship Lollipop* as if everything is great. In reality, everything isn't great. We have murder, rape, terrorism, bigotry, suffering. I think forgiveness is the ability to look at life the way it is, to accept that it's not perfect, and to go on. It admits the problem, and it moves forward."

This works for either side of the equation, it seems to me: the acceptance that yesterday can't be changed and the willingness to allow a fresh start tomorrow. In the context of Chris's story, the archbishop's explanation crystalizes something I've been trying to get my head around for a long time. It resonates with me, this concept of forgiveness as a bargain we make with ourselves. When I give up the hope of a better past, making the choice to forgive, that forgiveness is not going to help or punish the other person. Forgiveness is for me. And this approach seems like the opposite of another old saying that's never resonated with me: *Forgive and forget.*

"If you slap me, I can forgive you, but I'll always remember it," the archbishop clarifies. "If I'm driving drunk and I kill somebody, I can't change that, but by true forgiveness, I can move on. Forgiveness means I integrate it into my life — that's part of who I am. I can become a new person and not let that take me over."

The analogy takes my breath away, because it takes me back to that vivid moment Chris described: *Let it go.* Forgiveness was a pact he made with himself, and the boy who killed Chris's family had to make that pact within himself as well. But I wonder if a kid that age would have had the capacity to get there if Chris had not led the way.

"Forgiveness is very powerful," says Archbishop Wester. "The trouble is, you can't be forgiven until you know you've sinned. If I don't admit that I slapped you, then I'll never get forgiveness. Some people come to a priest to confess their sins, but they never confess their sins; they confess somebody else's. They blame the other person. You know, they say, 'My husband did this' or 'My wife did that.' So I say, 'Okay, tell your husband or wife to come to confession.' "

This also resonates with me. I can immediately think of two people who are guilty of the worst crimes imaginable but have never acknowledged the slightest wrongdoing. I'm often asked, "Have you forgiven your captors?" My answer is yes. Yes, I have. But I've never known how to explain to people that my forgiving them doesn't mean that I'd ever invite them into my home for Sunday dinner. In fact, I hope I go the rest of my life without ever seeing or speaking to them again. It makes a difference, I think, that the teenage driver who took the lives of Chris's family did something irresponsible with horrific, unintended consequences about which he felt crushing remorse, whereas Mitchell and Barzee carefully planned the harm they did to me. It was intentional and even somehow justified in their minds. Mitchell and Barzee — unlike Cameron White — have never expressed any remorse or a need to be forgiven. My forgiving them will not make a difference in how they live the rest of their lives. But it does make a difference for me. That's the point. If I were still holding on to the past, and dwelling on all of the terrible things they did to me all the time, they would be completely and wholly unaffected, but I would be destroying myself.

Forgiveness is not for the benefit of the other person; it's for yourself.

Thinking of it in the terms that Archbishop Wester used, it's much easier for me to explain: I can't change the fact that I was kidnapped, raped, held hostage for nine months. I'll never forget what happened to me. It changed me in many ways. But I can accept the fact that it happened, and I can choose to move on. I will never go back to being the same girl I was before I was kidnapped. What matters is the woman I choose to be now — and in the future — as I move forward.

Mom helped me see that after I was rescued. She didn't call it forgiveness at the time, but she led me toward that idea of forgiveness as giving up hope for a better past. I was in Mom's bedroom the morning after I returned home, and we were talking about all that had changed while I was gone. I was giving her a hard time because she hadn't folded my clothes in my closet. She'd left it exactly as I had, all messy and disorganized, as most fourteen-year-olds' closets would be.

As I went to take a shower, Mom said, "Elizabeth, what these people have done to you is terrible. There aren't words strong enough to describe how wicked and evil they are. They've stolen nine months of your life that you will never get back. The best punishment you could ever give them is to *be happy* — to move on and do exactly what you want. Because feeling sorry for yourself and holding on to what happened is only allowing them to steal more of your life away from you, and they don't deserve a single second more."

She went on to say that God is our ultimate judge, that He would make everything up to me that I'd lost, and that the people who'd hurt me would also receive their just reward. She said they should be happy for every day they are on earth, because it says in the Bible that if someone hurts a child, it's better for them to be at the bottom of the ocean with a millstone tied about their neck than to face God's wrath.

Her advice has stayed with me ever since that day. I think I realized even then that she was right. My captors don't care how I feel. If I am as miserable and as unhappy as they are, so much the better for them. The best thing I can do is accept that there were things taken from me — time, innocence, my safe and peaceful childhood — precious things that I will never get back. Now I have to move on to live my life the best way I know how.

None of us is perfect or will have a perfect life. No doubt we all struggle with something. But to live with the realization that forgiveness is for ourselves means that we can actually use that powerful healing tool in our lives. We will always have problems and struggles and failures, but we will also have hope and knowledge that we can always move forward. So as tragic as Chris's story is, I find it equally hopeful. We can come back. We can forgive and be forgiven.

A few years ago, I had the opportunity to be included in creating an online class on psychology. I'm certainly no expert on the subject, but the other person involved was Dr. Paul Jenkins, the author of *The Love Choice* and *Pathological Positivity,* who readily affirms that he is "a man of faith" and that his faith brings both context and meaning to his work. We became good friends, and he said he'd be happy to answer my questions about his practice and about the psychology of resilience and hope in general. (More about that later.) It wasn't my intention to ask him about forgiveness per se, but we end up spending quite a lot of time on the topic. His take on forgiveness is quite straightforward: "Snakes are going to be snakes. Forgiveness is about acknowledging that the snake is a snake, and if it bites you, you're not going to chase it down. You're going to focus on getting the venom out of your system."

I like that analogy too.

"It's really a healing gift that we give ourselves," says Dr. Paul. "It has nothing to do with the other person. I had a client who was thirty-two, I think, when she came to see me. Single. Had an eight-year-old daughter. She was about 150 pounds overweight and depressed. We got to the part about forgiveness, and she almost fired me when I brought up that concept. Her stepfather had sexually molested her from the time she was eight years old until she was sixteen. Constant sexual abuse over that period of eight years, and he never even acknowledged that it was wrong. He never apologized. Forgiveness — can you see why she didn't want to go there? Now, to put context around this, her stepfather had died ten years earlier. Elizabeth, what if she forgives him? What difference is it going to make to his life?"

"None. None at all."

"Exactly. And what's it doing to her to hang on to it?"

"It's killing her," I answer, with sadness for the reality of that.

"And not only her. She's got an eight-year-old daughter. Who else is it hurting?"

"Probably everyone close to her."

"Everyone who loves her or has any kind of connection to her," Dr. Paul agrees. "But it's not making a hill of beans of difference to her stepfather."

"Just so I'm clear, Dr. Paul, you would definitely say — and I feel like, myself included in this — many of us grow up with this idea that forgiveness somehow goes both ways, but really, it's a one-way street."

"It's a choice," says Dr. Paul. "And it can happen today."

I think that choice presents itself to us in the form of three critical questions:

Am I ready to accept the past?

What is the day — the hour, the *now* — when I fulfill that promise to myself and *let it go*?

And how will I integrate what's happened into who I choose to become in the future?

10
Something Worth Striving For

Far away there in the sunshine are my highest aspirations. I may not reach them, but I can look up and see their beauty, believe in them, and try to follow where they lead.

— Louisa May Alcott

I attended the Suzuki harp camp every summer when I was growing up. Sometimes it was down in Provo on one of the university campuses, and sometimes it was up at the Park City junior high school. There were group classes, master classes, private lessons, and lots of personal practice time. It was something I always looked forward to. My mom would come with me and spend the whole day with me in my classes and then practicing. That was a rare treat. When my sister, Mary Katherine, got older, she would attend the camp with me, and my mom would split her time between my classes and my sister's.

At the end of the week, everyone who attended would play in a concert together for all the parents and friends who wanted to come. It was during one of those summer camps that I first heard my mom talk about the Aspen Music Festival and School, nestled high in the Colorado mountains. After I heard her talk about it, I knew that I wanted to go. It was a long time before that actually happened. It was five years after I was rescued, and I had just finished my freshman year at Brigham Young University. I had never practiced so hard, long, or diligently in my life. Four hours a day of solid practicing had really made a difference in my playing.

During the year, I had decided that I wanted to apply to Aspen. Miracles of miracles, I was accepted, and I even got a partial scholarship. I was so excited. I couldn't wait to attend. Another student in the harp department — my friend Jenna, who had also just completed her freshman year — had also been accepted. (As the harp department consisted of only eight harpists, I knew them all and fortunately was friends with them all.) Jenna and I arranged to live together in the dorms close to the Aspen campus. Jenna was not only a talented harpist, she was also beautiful and had fashion-able clothing. She's the kind of person who seems so perfect you want to dislike her, but you can't because she is so kind.

The day before my dad drove my harp and me out to Aspen, I was desperately begging my mom to let me take her mountain bike with me to use. Unfortunately, I think my youngest brother, William, had the inside track with her on her bike. He had learned early how to ride a two-wheeler without training wheels and had basically claimed my mom's bike as his own. I hadn't had a bike since I'd grown out of my last one years earlier. Despite my begging and pleading, my mom would not cave. She said that her friend had a "lady's cruiser" that she would let me take. I was nonplussed by the idea. I was going to the high mountains for the summer, not to the beach. I needed a mountain bike. Mom won, of course. She and Dad picked up the "lady's cruiser" from her friend and brought it home.

All my worst fears were confirmed. The bike was a rust bucket, the black foamy stuff on the handlebars disintegrated every time you touched it, and the brakes didn't work. I wasn't even sure if the seat was *sit*able; it looked like it had to be at least fifty years old and had probably spent that amount of time in the gutter. Dad started tinkering away on it, trying to get it in riding shape. At this point, some of you might be wondering, "Why didn't she just go out and buy a new bike?" That is an easy question to answer: I was broke. My parents always believed in the importance of teaching my siblings and me how to work. The school semester had ended shortly before Aspen was due to start, and I had spent every second I could working as a teller at Wells Fargo to make sure I had enough to pay for Aspen and to make it through the summer. I didn't know what I was going to do about school in the fall, but I figured I'd cross that bridge when I came to it. I didn't have the money to pay for Aspen and a new bike, so I had to settle for the rust bucket.

We drove all the next day and finally arrived in Aspen. As we were unloading the car, I realized that we didn't have a bike lock — not that anyone would steal my rust bucket, but someone might think it was abandoned or junk, and then I would be without any type of bike. I told my dad before he left, and he said, "Not to worry. I have something in the car that might work."

Next thing I knew, he was walking back with a twelve-foot snowmobile cable and lock. I almost wanted to cry. The crappiest bike by far among the student population now had the most protection. The cable had to be wrapped around the bars of the bike and wrapped so many times that it almost appeared to be more cable than bike. This seemed like overkill for a bike no one would steal unless they wanted to shove it down a gulley to see what would happen. As soon as my dad left, I quickly walked inside and tried to pretend that the monstrosity chained up outside my door wasn't mine. When Jenna arrived a short while later, her parents helped her unload, wheeling out a completely respectable bike — probably one of the nicest bikes among the student population — and locking it up with a normal, nonobtrusive bike lock, next to mine.

I loved my time in Aspen — the lessons, the concerts. I cried my eyes out when the opera *Madama Butterfly* was performed. Studying with world-renowned teachers and playing under great conductors was a once-in-a-lifetime opportunity for me. Jenna and I biked everywhere, and I eventually got to where I could reasonably cohabit with my bike. The Maroon Bells, the mountains up the canyon from our dorms, are said to be some of the most photographed mountains in the United States. They are breathtaking.

It was about eleven miles, all uphill, from the dorms to the top of the canyon, where we'd be able to really look up at the Maroon Bells. Jenna and I would often ride part of the way up the canyon and then turn around to zoom back down to the dorms. One day, we decided that we would see how far we could get before turning around.

We started riding, and things were all right at first, but the further we went, the harder it became. My bike had a very limited gear range, and I was in the easiest gear already, almost from the beginning. I kept waiting for Jenna to say she was ready to turn around, but she kept going. I couldn't even detect the slightest degree of effort on her part. Her feet just kept pedaling as easily as if we were on flat land. My legs were screaming out in agony, and I couldn't help but think this was all my mom's fault. There were some other thoughts that went through my mind that aren't appropriate to share.

At one point, I finally overcame my pride for half a second and asked Jenna if she was ready to turn around yet. She smiled and looked back at me and said, "We've never come this far before. I'm going to keep going to the top, but don't feel like you need to keep going if you don't want to."

Well, that was it. I had to keep going.

I thought, rather uncharitably, *I survived nine months of being kidnapped and held hostage. What has she ever survived? If she is going to finish it, I am bloody well going to finish it.* I continued to struggle and struggle. If I went too slow, the flies would swarm me; if I went much faster, I really didn't know if my legs would hold out. When we finally made it to the top, I wasn't sure if I was going to have diarrhea or throw up. Neither happened, fortunately. I just stood there, sweating and panting, looking up at the Maroon Bells, trying to decide if they were worth it. The ride down was pitifully short. We rode so fast, I feared for my life, which now depended on brakes that weren't at all what you would call dependable.

We both made it back to our dorm, and I was a little the worse for wear, but I'm happy to say that I did finish the ride. This certainly was no life-altering moment, no great triumph or tragedy, but I look back and laugh now whenever I think of it. It serves as a reminder to myself that once I have chosen a path, I need to keep going. There will always be good reasons to stop — fatigue, flies, pain — but the end result is worth it. Life is meant to be full of struggle. We are meant to be challenged, and even when we reach the top of one summit, there will always be another.

I like to feel myself progress. I like to mark my progress, and one of the clearest ways for me to do that is to set goals. More often than not, I bite off more than I can chew, but even if I don't complete my goal as originally hoped, I am able to see the progress, and to me that's what is important.

Mike Schlappi's entire life is an example of setting and achieving goals. It's also an example of overcoming some of the most daunting obstacles that could possibly stand between a goal and its achievement.

When Mike was a young teenager, he stopped by his good friend Tory's house. They'd planned to walk together to football practice. Mike was a star athlete and his father's pride. While the two boys were at Tory's house, Tory picked up his father's off-duty police revolver and emptied the magazine. He thought the gun was completely empty of bullets, but there was still one in the chamber. Tory, standing only three feet away from Mike, pulled the trigger.

In one hundredth of a second, Mike's life was permanently changed. The bullet that sped from the gun punctured a lung, clipped his heart, and embedded itself in his spine. Tory panicked and started screaming and crying. Mike lay on the bed, realizing that he had been shot and was in very critical condition. He knew he would die if he didn't receive medical help immediately. He did his best to calm Tory down and have Tory call his mom. Mike's mom showed up a few minutes later, as did the emergency crews to take him to the hospital.

He was told in the hospital that if he was ever going to walk again, the sensation would come back into his legs sooner rather than later. The sensation never returned. Mike has been a paraplegic since that day. But that didn't stop him from winning three Olympic medals.

The first time I met Mike, we went to Olive Garden and had a great time chatting. This was early in my quest, but I was getting better at asking the questions that opened doors and got me thinking. Unfortunately, I was still getting used to the technology side of recording and uploading interviews. I was depending on a smartphone app that, I discovered later, tends to be a little glitchy. Somewhere between the phone and the computer, the conversation disappeared. I felt like an idiot when I called Mike and asked him if I could talk to him again because the miracle of technology had failed me. I went out that day and bought a digital recorder. I wasn't going to take any more chances; I would record the interview on both my phone and on my new recorder. Mike was as polite and accommodating as is possible. He told me it would be a pleasure to go to lunch with me again and chat, and we set a date for the following week.

The morning arrives, and I'm not sure why this is, but whenever I'm about to get together with somebody, my life always seems to become a bit chaotic. Matthew, in a rush to meet with some of his clients, is unable to watch Chloé while I meet with Mike, so I quickly fill her diaper bag with animal crackers, toys, and her bottle, hoping that'll be enough to entertain her through lunch and my conversation with Mike at a Thai food place. I arrive a few minutes early — which almost never happens to me since having a child — and Chloé seems content to drop crackers on the floor and stick her little hand in my water glass while we're waiting.

Then Mike rolls in, and he has the biggest grin on his face when he sees my little Chloé. After we struggle through the meal with Chloé trying to escape her stroller every two seconds, there's more chicken and vegetables down her front than in her tummy. Mike suggests we go back to his house, where there are lots of toys, his two little dogs, and his wife for Chloé to play with while we chat. I gratefully accept. I'm continually amazed by and thankful for the way people I've asked to interview have welcomed me into their homes and into their lives.

It's a hot summer day, and the interior of Mike's home is nice and cool. His wife begins pulling out all sorts of toys for Chloé, whose attention is immediately caught, until she sees the little dogs. After that, all she wants to do is chase the dogs around and try to pick them up. While they play, Mike invites me into his study, and I ask him, "Was there one person or maybe a few people who influenced your life after you were shot? Someone who encouraged you to keep going?"

"There's probably four or five that really stand out," he says. "I'll just clump my family into one. Brothers and sisters that cared for me. Mom loved me no matter what, disabled or not. I knew it, felt it. Dad — it was hard for him, but still he kicked me in the butt and made me deal with this and get over it and move on. So my family, definitely. Mike Johnson, another guy in a wheelchair, lost his legs in Vietnam. He came and visited me in the hospital. It impacted me, because I'm like, 'Hey, you're married. You drove over here. You're in a wheelchair, and you're okay.' It gave me a role model. I also had some very good friends who made me feel very loved and very normal."

"Mike, you're so . . . *happy.* You seem like you're always headed in a positive direction. Do you ever have bad days?"

"Well, yeah." Mike shrugs. "It's kind of a strange concept, but I like the concept that your attitude is not your mood. Everybody in life, when you're having a bad day or something's happened to you — a tragedy — some people are going to say to you, 'Oh, get over it,' or 'Change your attitude,' or 'Stay positive.' That's not always healthy. You need to process it. You need to go through it. I got shot, and if I had just immediately said, 'Oh, I'm fine. This didn't happen. I'm not going to have a bad day. I'll fake it,' I wouldn't be healthy. I had to go through those moments, those days, those weeks. That is your mood. It's your feelings. You're depressed. That's real. That's good. Your attitude is your position in life. The best way I can describe it is, attitude is a position, like an airplane has an attitude indicator that measures the plane's position to the horizon. That's where they're headed. Just like the plane, you can have a bad mood but still be in the correct position. It really hit me strongly because I used to think, *I gotta snap out of it.*"

I'm not sure why I find this comforting, but I do. Of course, I don't want anyone to have a bad day. It's just good to know I'm not alone. I ask him, "Do you think it's possible to be in a negative mood and still be going in a positive direction?"

"Sure. I can have a bad day and still be heading in the right direction. When something bad happens, you have the right to those feelings, but get positioned for a positive future. *Believe* you'll get through it. *Act* as if you're going to get through it. *Live* as if everything is going to turn out good."

That strikes me as such a direct way of living. Such a straightforward trajectory: Believe. Act. Live. "But how do you physically do that?" I wonder out loud.

"The first thing to *get over it,*" says Mike, "is just believe you can. Make a decision that you will get over it. I'm in a wheelchair. I remember the first curb that I saw — little six-inch curb you can step right up and walk on — and that looked like a cliff to me, but I thought, *I'm going to pop a wheelie, and*

I'm going to get my front wheels up on top of that curb, and I'm going to get my momentum going, and I'm going to get up on top of that curb. I'm going to get over it and get on with my life. You have to make the decision that you are going to do everything you can to move forward. I'm not going to say you don't have bad days. You wouldn't be normal if you never experienced a setback. It is just a conscious decision every day that *I can do this.*"

Throughout our whole conversation, Mike has had a smile on his face. Even when he told me about his friend shooting him. And the weird thing about that is that it is not weird at all. The smile isn't a positive attitude mask; it's a natural, easygoing smile. Mike isn't one of those people who are constantly forcing themselves to be so happy that it gets saccharine. He is just naturally happy, organically positive, and very genuine. Nothing comes off as plastic or pretend. He has to adjust his legs and seat every few minutes; it's clear he lives every day in a lot of pain.

"How is it possible to stick with all that when you live with so much physical pain?"

"I do have my grumpy days," he assures me, "but as a kid I had the nickname Happy Schlappi. Maybe I just tried to live up to that label. Life is hard, whether it hits you at fourteen or fifty, but the biggest difference for me is finding the things to be grateful for. We have so much to be grateful for — the beauty around us, our families, our bodies, our friends, our dogs. It comes from my mother, to be able to see the good in all situations. Even after I was shot, I was focusing on what I had left instead of what I had lost. I'm thankful I'm alive. My heart was on an in-beat when I got shot or else I'd be dead. My mom still loves me. God still loves me. My arms work. It gets harder. I live in a lot of physical pain. It hurts, and I'm not going to deny taking a painkiller once in a while, but sports have been good for that, because when I move around, it takes all those nerve-ending pains. What it comes down to is, I'm not in control of my pain, but I'm in charge of the way I react to it."

Mike's determination and positivity helped him to achieve so much, from surviving in the hospital to learning how to get over a curb in a wheelchair. It's interesting because when I first met him, to me his story seemed to be about getting shot and then going to the Olympics three times. I mean, come on! That's a great story. But now that I'm here, talking with Mike the human being as opposed to Mike the hero-on-paper, it seems to me that getting over the six-inch curb required a different kind of heroism.

Still, the Olympics are a pretty big deal, so I feel compelled to ask about that, and when I do, Mike's face lights up.

"I just love sports. I was a basketball guy, and I was supposed to be a star basketball player in high school and college. Now I'm in a wheelchair and disabled, but then when I found out they had wheelchair basketball in the Olympics, I wondered, *Is that like Special Olympics?* No, this is the real Olympics, but for people with physical disabilities, not intellectual disabilities. That got into my blood. I started playing, and I became good at it; I tried out for the national team. I was on four different Olympic teams. Got a couple medals. It was good. When they put the gold medal around my neck in Seoul in '88, I was the youngest on the team, and I just started crying because it's like, *Wait a minute. I was lying in a hospital bed ten years ago. My dad, my coach, thought I'd never play sports again, and now I'm doing more than high school, more than college.* I was able to take this thing that seemed so negative and, with the right perspective and framing it properly, it became a good thing."

"A *great* thing," I remind him. "You are someone who has achieved *great*ness. You've gone to the Olympics. You've been inducted into the Basketball Hall of Fame. People might look at you and think you are the exception. What would you say to someone going through a difficult time if maybe they don't see themselves as exceptional?"

"You're okay. You're normal. You're real. This is an opportunity. Let me rephrase that." He thinks it over for a moment before he clarifies, "This is an opportunity *to grow*. To learn about your character. To go to other people for help. To rip down the wall around you. It'll be hard, and that's okay. You'll have feelings, and that's okay. Always believe, always know that you can get through this with help. *With help.* Not alone. That's too hard. We need help."

The interview came to an end, and I think Mike's two dogs were happy to see the back of me and Chloé, knowing that their little tormentor was leaving. But my conversation with Mike left me feeling uplifted and empowered, like I could accomplish any-thing — including wrangling a toddler and an infant. Mike is that example of making up his mind to do something and then, no matter what, finding a way to accomplish it.

Mike showed me that whatever our circumstances, we need to see ourselves headed in a positive direction, pursuing a positive goal, no matter where we are in life. I think I knew this already, but to hear it articulated this way helped confirm to me that we still can be headed in a positive direction even if we aren't happy. Even when we're struggling.

I suppose I could try to make a parallel here about my bike ride, and refusing to stop or give up, but really, the main area where I set goals for myself — and strive to achieve them — is my music. It's something that allows me to measure my progress. I love that feeling of falling in love with a new piece I've never heard before, getting the music, practicing it until I'm sick of hearing it, learning the nuances in the music, the subtle melodies interwoven throughout the work, and finally being able to perform it at a high level. Either I can play it beautifully or I'm working toward playing it beautifully.

I began playing the harp when I was only five years old. It seemed like a magical instrument, the instrument of angels. When I first started, I would imagine myself in a beautiful gown onstage performing to a large audience. My first teacher taught me so much, until I was eighteen, to be precise.

I grew up learning the Suzuki Method, which taught me to really listen to the music. My mom would buy a CD of the piece I was supposed to learn, and I would listen to it over and over and over. From an early age, this taught me to appreciate music, and made me want to listen to classical music.

I remember finding a CD of Tchaikovsky's *The Nutcracker* and racing up and down the halls listening to it, just feeling the music and trying to dance around to it. I remember when I learned the first piece that I considered advanced: Carlos Salzedo's "Chanson dans la Nuit" (Song in the Night), with its tumbling glissandos and built-in percussion that make the most of both the strings and the wooden frame of the instrument. I really thought I had achieved greatness. I competed in small local competitions and felt so excited when I won. Outside my teacher's studio, when people would say, "Introduce yourself and tell us something about yourself," I would always say, "My name is Elizabeth Smart, and I play the harp." I felt so special and proud saying that. Rarely did anyone else say they played the harp. Before I was kidnapped, I felt that my harp playing defined me, in and outside of school and within my family. That was what I did. I know that my mom can attest to that because she sat through every lesson I ever had until I turned sixteen and she finally decided that I was old enough to go by myself. My mom probably felt like her life was raising her children and harp. She didn't play, but she was my biggest fan and motivator.

During those long months of captivity, I wasn't allowed to speak of the harp, but my captors couldn't keep me from thinking about it, dreaming of the day I'd feel my fingers on the strings again. I had to hold on to that sliver of myself. *My name is Elizabeth Smart, and I play the harp.* After I was rescued, I was excited to go back to playing the harp. I was looking forward to feeling those same feelings. I resumed my harp lessons, but when I eventually made it back to school that following fall, I quickly fell into the drama that is high school, and although harp was still a major part of my life, I became distracted by homework, friends, boys, and driving. I had always planned to study music in college. My dream was to go to Juilliard, but as the time to start applying to colleges drew near, I realized that Juilliard was not realistic for me, and that unless I really got serious about my practicing,

I wouldn't be able to go anywhere for music.

So I got serious about my practicing. I decided I wanted to go to Brigham Young University; it had an excellent music program and had spent years building up its harp program. The day of my audition, a cold snowy day in January, I was required to perform two pieces and one étude, after which I would have to take an aural test. My mom sat outside the room as I performed inside. I actually can't remember at all how I played. I knew both of the judges personally, but I can't remember if I walked out of that room feeling confident or worried. I took the aural test, which to this day I have no idea how I passed. The test consisted of listening to different notes and rhythms being played and choosing from several options to correctly identify them.

Mom had left after the performance part of the audition, and my boyfriend at the time was going to drive me the fifty miles back to my home. As soon as the test was complete, I looked down at my phone and saw I had missed several phone calls from my family. I quickly called them back and asked, "What's going on?"

Grandpa Smart was dying. They told me that if I ever wanted to see him again, I needed to get there fast. He had checked out of the hospital that morning, knowing he was going to check out of life. I had always been very close to Grandpa Smart. He was the one who taught me to love horses, riding, and late-night snowmobile adventures. I needed to be there to say good-bye before he died. I rushed to get my boyfriend and told him what was going on. He was a complete gentleman and started the car immediately. We raced off down the road, but by this time, the snowy day had progressed into a full-blown whiteout. Cars were backed up for miles on the freeway, moving at a snail's pace. I worried I wasn't going to make it. All the stress of the audition melted out of my mind — which is probably why I still can't remember how I felt after the performance part.

I did finally make it to my grandparents' home, about two blocks away from mine. As I ran in through the door, Grandpa Smart took another breath and then another, though each one seemed like a lot of work. I was able to tell him that I loved him so much. I said good-bye. My harp had appeared. Someone had brought it in so I could play one of the pieces that I had auditioned with: "Contemplation" by Henriette Renié. It is a beautiful, peaceful work, and as I played, my grandfather passed away. I hope he heard it before he went on to hear the true heavenly harps play. I always felt he waited for me to make it there, waited for me to say good-bye.

It wasn't until a few days later that I wondered how I had fared at the audition. Would I be accepted? Would I be rejected? What would I do if I was rejected? Audition again next year? Try something new? I received my acceptance letter a few weeks later, and I was so excited that I was going to study harp performance, something I was good at. Professor Nicole Brady had recently been appointed director of the harp program. My freshman year was her first year teaching at a university.

Under Professor Brady's tutelage I learned and progressed rapidly, better and faster than I ever had before. She inspired me, and I felt like I could accomplish anything. I always felt she believed in me, which made me believe that I had the ability to learn and play anything as long as I practiced hard enough. When I think of people who have inspired me to reach farther and achieve more, I think of her. I knew her before I studied under her, and I still consider her a mentor and dear friend to this day. So when I decided to write this book, she was on my list of people to interview from the beginning. I was thinking, even before Mike Schlappi helped me articulate it, that an essential part of healing, of hope, is having a goal that pulls us in a positive direction — like a lighthouse that gives us something to steer toward through storm and fog.

I drive to Nicole's home, and as I pull up, I feel a little rush of excitement looking at her front door. Nicole has achieved the highest degree of education a person can get, studied under one of the greatest harp teachers in the world in Moscow and got a doctorate from Juilliard.

When I ask her what it was that drove her to achieve at that level, she says, "I loved school. When I was little, my dad always asked us, 'What do you want to be when you grow up?' We always had to have something to say. We could change it the next day, but we always had to have something to say. That was a direction giver for my life, always having a plan. I was also one of those kids that loved quotes like, 'Aim for the clouds because at least you'll hit the treetops.' I felt like if I could take my education as far as I could, I would be able to help others through teaching. That mattered so much to me, helping others, and teaching seemed the way to do that."

"How would you say music affects you?"

"I guess I would say there have been times in my life when it has really saved me," says Nicole. "I find it a really helpful thing now, when I feel my life is so chaotic with my four boys, that I can go and there's this place of peace. Even if I'm stressed-out about a performance I have to play or something, I always find peace there."

"When I was a student, I always felt like you understood what was going on in my life so well. I always felt like you adjusted your teaching style to meet what I needed at the time. Do you do that with every student?"

"Music instruction is one-on-one, which allows for lots of connection between people. It is also very personal. Everyone enters at their own level, and it's very subjective. Because of that, you have to adapt to each student. The teacher that can't do that isn't a very good teacher, because it's a very important part of being a teacher."

"Being a teacher — being *my* teacher — you were always able to encourage me and inspire me to want to conquer whatever I was struggling with whenever I came in feeling like I had hit a wall or things just weren't connecting. How did you do that?"

"I want my students to learn music they

love. They're motivated if they love it. Sometimes when a student comes to me with a piece in mind, I might recommend another before that piece to help prepare them in their technique or playing so they are able to confidently learn and play their desired piece. More than anything, I want them to love what they are doing."

Thinking back on my time under Nicole as a student at BYU almost makes me wish I were still there. There was nothing like going to a lesson knowing I had practiced my brains out and was prepared, setting new goals for the next week, feeling so excited to go out and tackle them. I learned so much, not just about music but about myself. I learned that I have a tendency to bite off more than I can chew, and no matter how many times I do that to myself and have to readjust my goals, I will once again bite off more than I can chew. I almost laughingly ask Nicole, "How do you make realistic goals for yourself? Please, tell me the secret!"

"I keep a practice journal," she says. "I have done this specifically with harp, but it would probably be good to do with the rest of my life. The first thing is to write what you're going to do in your practice session. What you're going to accomplish. And then at the bottom of the page, at the end of your practice session, write if you did accomplish what you had written. Then compare the two — what you wanted and what you did — so you can set better goals next time. Usually our goal making is off, too high or too low. So if I have a student who wants to compete in a competition or something, I tell them to set a drop-dead date before the competition, and if they're not ready by that drop-dead date, then forget it. You are not going to that competition. It helps my students to be realistic."

It's comforting for me to hear someone I look up to say that our goal making is usually off. Every New Year's Eve, I write a whole list of plans and new goals I'm going to achieve that year. I'm probably not alone in that. Every year, I feel lucky if I achieve even a quarter of what I had written down. I'm probably not alone in that either. Life does happen, and life does get in the way, but it's important to continually set goals for ourselves and make the daily choice to pursue them to whatever extent we can.

Nicole Brady, whose words affected me even more than her harp instruction, helped me realize that what it comes down to is our desire to progress, our desire to move forward. Goals don't have to be big. They don't have to have anything to do with music, basketball, or anything else in particular. Sometimes the goal is getting through the day. I know what it's like to want to stay in bed and hide under the covers. Sometimes the worthy goals are simple and achievable tasks like "Get out of bed today," or "Do laundry," or "Do something to make myself happy." Each goal we achieve is a step, a choice to move forward. To take one more breath. And then take another.

I have always said, "It's not what happens to us that defines who we are, it's our choices that define who we are."

Mike Schlappi exemplifies this philosophy. He continually chose to think beyond the wheelchair and focus on doing all that he wanted to do. But he also chose to be happy. For people like me, who are always aiming a little too high, the temptation is to judge ourselves or compare ourselves to others who've gotten to the place we hope to go. But if happiness is the most important goal, doesn't self-judgment take us a step backwards?

If our goals guide us and give us something to strive for, can we find happiness in the pursuit and be okay with the idea that we may never actually reach the goal?

Do our goals give our lives purpose — or is purpose something larger?

11
LIVING WITH A PURPOSE

I am not what happened to me. I am what I choose to become.

— CARL JUNG

If we wait for someone else to fix our problems, they probably will never be fixed. Whether we find ourselves with an actual number on the days of life we have left or we just realize that we all have a limited amount of time, we need to make sure we don't squander our life here. You've heard that old saying "In the end, it's not the years in your life that count. It's the life in your years." It's all about *why* we're living, not just how. It's about loving this life that could so easily pass us by if we live passively.

Alec Unsicker, along with his family, started AJU Foundation, putting Alec's initials and the family's personal spin on "Make a Wish," with a simple purpose: "To put smiles on the faces of people battling cancer." A smile may not seem like such a grand purpose in the big picture, but as a teenager coping with cancer since childhood, Alec sees the big picture a bit differently.

In the very first texts I exchanged with Alec, he was happy, positive, and willing to help me. We set a time and date for me to drive the hour and a half from my house to his, to interview him for an hour or so. This may not seem like a lot to most people, but when you are told you have a limited amount of time to live, each hour is precious and makes a difference. I was grateful for the opportunity to spend time with Alec and his family.

On the drive up to Alec's home, it's so windy I can feel my car being blown, which is pretty significant because I drive a heavy-duty SUV to deal with the snowfall in the Utah winter. When I get out of the car at his home in a quiet neighborhood, I have a Marilyn Monroe moment with the wind blowing my dress up. Thank goodness no one is around to see it. I walk up to the front door, which immediately opens, and Alec's mom, Sunny, welcomes me into their home. Alec is small and pale with close-cropped blond hair. There's a reserved feeling about him, but his smile is broad and genuine, and he's pretty much always smiling. He sits on the sofa with his back to the window. I know he's just turned eighteen, but he looks no older than thirteen. He's quiet and a bit shy, but "the spirit is willing," as that old saying goes; he has a certain energy that feels open and fresh when he tells me he's happy to meet me and ready to answer any question I have.

My first question, which is probably everyone's first question, is meant to get the housekeeping out of the way: "What kind of cancer do you have? And when were you diagnosed?" When I hear the words, they feel so blunt. I realize I've asked him to put his experience in a nutshell in the very way I hate to do with my own experience. But Alec looks at me and, without a trace of annoyance, rattles off the well-practiced details.

"Medulloblastoma. It was a brain tumor. I was diagnosed when I was eleven. I had been throwing up for a couple of months. We had no idea why. They started all different kinds of tests on my stomach, and then I started getting headaches. The doctors performed an MRI, which revealed that I had a tumor on the back of my head, and whenever I threw up it relieved pressure, which is why I kept throwing up. That was three days before my birthday. They operated on my birthday and took out the tumor on my birthday, so that was fun."

"Wow, what a birthday present."

"Yeah. They gave me a cupcake, but my dad ate it! I was like, 'They just had to tell me that.' It was really funny."

"Did they get the whole tumor?"

"No, there was just a little bit left in my brain stem. They got rid of the rest. I went through about a year of chemo and radiation. Radiation first, for like a month and a half. Then every month, every five weeks, I went in for a week of chemo in the hospital, and we did that for a year. Then we got an MRI after that, and it looked like everything was clean and done. The MRI showed that everything had done its job, and I was cancer free. I just kept on with my life"

"You were in fifth grade then?"

"Yeah," he says, and I see in his eyes how far away it seems now. "Fifth grade."

"Were you still going to school?"

"I didn't go to school. I went in at the end of every year and took tests. And I was fine, which is kind of funny."

"Naturally brilliant," I tease, and Alec laughs, agreeing readily with that diagnosis.

"In sixth grade, my teacher came over twice a week to teach me the basic stuff they learned, and that was really helpful. She's like my best friend now."

"Did having cancer change you a lot? Before you got cancer, were you into sports or computers or . . . ?"

"I was more active before I had cancer, but I always liked reading books and playing video games. But when I returned to school in my seventh-grade year, after they told me I was cured, I just couldn't do it. I could, but I would stop in the middle and sometimes go to the bathroom and just throw up for a little bit and then come back out. I was just throwing up because I'd done it for two years."

As if seventh grade isn't hard enough on a guy. The changes at that age — like getting my first period in the worst possible conditions. I think there's an added layer of stuff when an adolescent is plunged into a life-threatening situation. It's difficult to determine where the normal challenge of growing up begins when the challenge of staying alive is so overwhelming.

"Alec, did you ever feel angry or upset over being ill?"

"No. I never got that feeling. I wasn't ever angry. Sometimes I would get depressed, but my mom helped a lot, and my dad and family. They were always there. I had cousins and friends who always wanted to come say hi."

"But then . . ."

"Well, I still had to go in at first every three months for another MRI, then every six months, and eventually every year. It was in the middle of my sophomore year of high school when we were going in for our last MRI to be done. If it was a clean slate, we would get to go home and probably never have to see them again. But then they found tumors of the same thing, medulloblastoma, in the base of my spine. I was pretty devastated. When we got home, I went straight to my room and cried for five minutes, and then I was okay."

Alec is so matter-of-fact about just going into his room and crying for five minutes, I have to ask, "Just five minutes?"

Alec turns to Sunny to back him up. "Would you say five minutes?"

"Maybe ten," says Sunny.

"Okay," he concedes, "maybe ten."

"That's it?" I smile. "My goodness."

"I listened to my music and stuff."

"What kind of music do you like?"

"The Beatles," he says. "The one I listened to while I was up there crying — *ob-la-di ob-la-da, life goes on* — that just helped me."

"What were the doctors telling you at that point?"

"They said, 'We're going to do more radiation, more chemo, and hopefully that will bring it down.' We did chemo for like six months, and every time we went back for MRIs, they said it wasn't changing at all, but toward the end, we went to see the radiologist, and he was all upbeat and happy about it. He said we had only been comparing the scans with the previous most recent scan, which showed little or no change, but then he compared it to the original scan, and said, 'There's a huge difference. The tumors look a lot smaller now.' When we finished radiation, we were feeling really good. The radiologist thought he could really beat the tumors down, and then we went back for an MRI, and it turned out there were more tumors up and down in my spine. I haven't had any symptoms lately, but sooner or later, I will lose the use of my legs."

"What's the prognosis now?"

"My mom has looked up many alternative ways to help shrink the tumors, and we've been doing a couple of those. We haven't had an MRI lately, but I haven't had any symptoms, so we're pretty much just waiting."

I glance at Sunny to see if she has anything she'd like to add, but she's focused on Alec, listening.

"This state of not knowing," I say, directing the question to either or both of them, "how does it make you feel?"

"It made me feel kind of nervous at first," says Alec, "and then I just accepted it, and I could laugh because no one knows, so it made it funny."

"It's funny?" I echo. That was definitely not what I was expecting to hear.

"Well, not funny in the sense —" Sunny begins, but Alec isn't about to let her off the hook.

"It is! Because nobody knows. They don't know. Why are they worried about me?"

"Ah. I get it." I look down at my notes, which are no help, because things have gone in a totally unexpected direction. "How do you remain so calm about all this, Alec? How do you keep your hope?"

"I don't know." He shrugs like any eighteen-year-old guy. "I've just accepted it, and if I can't walk, that's okay, I guess. We really don't know anything at this point. I could die. But I'm not scared to die. I know what's waiting on the other side, and that's something better."

I look over at Alec's mother. Sunny, like

her son, is sitting there so calmly and serenely, but she is his mother, and I know if she could, she would switch places with him in a heartbeat. Being a new mother, I wonder how Sunny is able to sit there so positive and calm, knowing that Alec's days may be numbered.

"No matter how things are," she says, "I think we climb over the novelty, and my life experiences before this taught me to trust in the Lord. I didn't always, but I wanted to. When this happened, I was ready. I can think back and see there were things that prepared me."

I see what she's saying from her perspective, but I look back and can't even imagine anything that could have prepared me for what I experienced. In fact, I guess I'm grateful for that, because the only thing that could have prepared me was either being a Navy SEAL or going through a lot of other terrible experiences. I'm glad my life before that was simple and happy. I do see, however, that my kidnapping prepared me for other aspects of my life. It's always a point of reference.

As Sunny is speaking, I glance at Alec's older brother, Braydon, who has quietly joined us. He has tears in his eyes, and that makes me notice that nobody else is crying.

I don't know how they do it. I would be a blubbering mess. Maybe they have cried all their tears out. Or maybe they've gotten very good at not crying. I don't know, and I'm not sure how to ask, so I turn to Alec's brother and ask, "What do you think about everything?"

Braydon looks at me like he's wanted to say this for a long time. "I think the scariest thing for me is — at least in my head — I don't know if it's going to happen, but from what I gather from the information I've read and what I've been told, he's got these tumors in his spine and we can't stop them. They're growing. Eventually they're going to start compromising his body, his legs, his feeling. He's going to use a wheelchair. I don't know if it's going to happen that way. I don't know if it's going to be quicker, but I hate to see him suffer and just have to drag on. It's difficult to see him get worse and worse progressively while I can't do anything about it. I kind of wish it was just quicker, but at the same time I want him to stick around. It's just hard to see him suffer, and we don't know how bad it's going to get before he dies."

For the first time since the beginning of the conversation, I feel like someone has hit the nail on the head, describing exactly how

I would feel. He brings some raw emotion to the discussion. We're all different, we all experience things differently, and it's helpful to see the varied ways in which emotion and pain are processed. It's a healthy reminder that each path is unique, and each one of us navigates our path in his or her own unique way.

I look back to Alec, who is still sitting there as calmly as ever, almost too calmly. I have an eighteen-year-old brother who can barely make it through an hour of church meetings without getting squirmy. And when all my brothers are around, whether he's being teased or praised, if the topic involves him, he definitely has something to say. One of the things that intrigues me most about Alec is that despite having so little time left in this mortal walk of life, he still thinks of others. With all the potential heaviness of the cancer conversation, he's a lot more interested in talking about the AJU Foundation.

"We just barely started it," he says, "and we're working on our first Smile Package. That's what we call them. Because people have been helping me so much with gifts, visits, and random things, I want to share that with other cancer patients so they feel happy, even if it's just for a second."

Alec's life is an example of the importance of finding purpose in life even if the time remaining may be brief. Alec started with himself, accepting his illness, his fate, whatever the road holds for him, but he has taken it and expanded it beyond himself. Reaching out to others who are suffering from cancer, simply trying to make them smile with his "smile packages." No matter how much or how little time you may have, the one thing you know for sure is that you have *now,* and that's where Alec and his family live.

"My dad and I just started making plans to do these fun things. Went to New Zealand about a month ago. That was amazing. Next week we're going to Disneyland with all the children. That's one of the fun things, then I'm taking my GED. If I pass, I'll do online college. We're going to New York with all my cousins, and I'm really excited. I'm just excited for stuff and keep going. If I fall down dead, then too bad for everybody else. I'm going to a better place. See you guys later."

"What do you think it's like?" I ask quietly. "The better place?"

"I believe that I'm going to go to Heaven, and I'm going to be with our Heavenly Father, Jesus Christ, and all my ancestors who have been cheering me on and helping me through this whole rough time. There will be a ton of people there that I know and love, and it's just going to be the best."

Sitting here listening to this young man who is so boylike in appearance speak so calmly about death, it's hard to imagine facing all this without his strength of faith. I have often thought about how I feel about death personally, and I have never been scared of it or worried about what comes next, but I think that's because of the faith in which I was raised. I wonder how many people, faced with a potentially terminal illness the way Alec is, share his feelings and attitude. In the past, I was never afraid of death for myself, but now I think about what would happen to the people I love. Immediately my thoughts turn to Chloé. If I died, would she ever know how much I love her? Would she remember me at all? Would she know how special and precious she is to me? All things that, rationally or irrationally, I worry about now.

By the time you read this, Alec might be gone, but his love, relationships, and influence won't be. I feel like a person has achieved immortality in some form when, like Alec, they leave an impression upon the world and are remembered. Alec's family and friends who have been there through his illness and stood by him and loved him will forever remember him, thereby giving him some sense of immortality.

My grandpa Charles Smart was one of my heroes and someone I wanted to be like. He was a medical doctor, specializing in cancer research. He was a man of few words; his actions always spoke louder to me than anything else. At his funeral, many people got up and shared how much my grandpa had influenced their life and how much service he had given, going above and beyond the call of duty. Among all the talks and memories shared, there were different quotes shared of things he used to say.

One I particularly remember: "We're all terminal."

At the time, it more or less went in one ear and out the other, but it must have stuck somewhere in between, because in the last few months, it has resurfaced in my thoughts. "We're all terminal." I suppose that can be interpreted in different ways. The initial thought is, *Well, yes, we will all die one day.* But knowing my grandpa and having observed the kind of life he lived and who he strived to be, I think he meant more than simply "We will all die one day." I think he meant "Don't waste your time; we have only so much before it's all over."

For me, I all too often think that doing the stack of dishes in my sink or the pile of laundry waiting to be washed and folded and having a home that looks like a model house is the most important thing. But at the end of everything, that's not what I want to be remembered for — Champion Dish Washer — and I feel there's so much more to being a good wife and mother and human being. One of my recent struggles is finding the balance between working, being a mom, and living life in general. I wouldn't be writing this book otherwise. I don't have all the answers. I wish I did. I do believe there is so much to be learned from those around us.

Someone I did not know well personally but who left an impression on me was a fellow missionary. (I'll call him Daniel here, to protect his privacy.) He had the brightest smile. He was smart, kind, and funny. Everyone seemed to like him. I never heard a bad word spoken about him. After he completed his mission, he came home, and not long after he returned, his Facebook posts started to change. Clearly, he was going through a hard time. Having just completed a strict LDS mission, he came home and made the difficult decision to come out as gay — and not everyone was ready to hear that. The more time that passed, the less contact he made with his former friends and colleagues from his time as a missionary. I'm sad now that I didn't make more of an effort to reach out to him.

In July, I looked on Facebook and there was a post inviting everyone to his funeral. I stared at the screen, thinking, *What? No. He's my age. That can't be right.* It was unclear whether his death had been accidental or suicide. When I arrived at his funeral, trying to slip in the back door, there was hardly a seat available. Daniel's kindness and smile had impacted so many people. I don't know all the challenges and demons he faced in his life, but clearly, as was proved by the attendance at his funeral, he touched so many lives. How could he have felt so adrift and alone while he was living? Would it have been any different if everyone there at the funeral had reached out to him before it was too late? Or was he in a place where he couldn't let people in?

I get the joke now. Why Alec thinks it's funny that no one knows when he'll die. Because he has chosen to live life more fully than people who take their time for granted. He looks outward, beyond himself, to help others, and he draws energy from their smiles. *Ob-la-di, ob-la-da, life goes on. . . .*

It's easy to think that unless we live the kind of life lived by those we remember from history books — like Abraham Lincoln, Eleanor Roosevelt, Rosa Parks, Martin Luther King Jr., or Gandhi — we won't leave an impact on the world. Alec Unsicker has impacted family, friends, and community through his foundation, his determination to keep going, and his unassuming kindness. Daniel impacted his family, friends, and even casual acquaintances (like me) through his kindness, his struggles, and his bright smile. We won't all go down in the history books, we won't all be remembered for generations and generations, but that doesn't mean we shouldn't make the most of the limited time we all have here in this life. It's important to always live each day as if it's numbered, and to be grateful for each additional day we're given.

Dr. Paul Jenkins (the author of *Pathological Positivity,* as I mentioned earlier) received his Ph.D. in psychology in 1995 and has been in private practice ever since. Walking into the building that houses his office, I see that his door is slightly ajar and decide I'll just poke my head in and see if he's ready.

Dr. Paul looks up with a broad smile. He's athletic and tan, like most people who make the most of life in the high-altitude sunshine here in Utah. He immediately invites me into his office. It's nothing extravagant or over the top, just comfortable and simple.

When I ask about the difference between traditional therapy and the positive psychology he practices, he gives me a long explanation, which in my head boils down to a glass-half-full sort of take on things. Instead of exploring the darkest episodes of life, he looks at the mental health spectrum with pathology and treatment on the left — "the sick end" — mental health in the middle, and the goal — "to be truly fit and thriving" — on the right.

"Basically," he says, "I have taken my practice from the left side of the spectrum to the right, and there's some overlap in the middle because everybody's got issues. I think many forms of depression, anxiety, relationship conflicts, or challenges that people face in life — that's the middle of the spectrum. I don't think that means that you're broken. Probably it means that you're human. Welcome to Earth."

As the hour unfolds, talking and chatting is so easy that I realize we are almost out of time and I've hardly touched on the questions in my notes.

"If it's not too personal: What have been some moments in your life when you have helped yourself with positive psychology?"

He considers it for a moment and says, "I got into a few investments that all hit south at the same time. I ended up filing for bankruptcy. It was hard for me to even admit that for a while, because I used to think people who go through a bankruptcy are either flakes or dishonest, or there's something wrong with their character. At the lowest point, I was walking out of the courtroom. I looked around, and the thing that surprised me the most was that everything was still in color. Somehow I expected it to be like one of those old 1920s movies where everything's black-and-white and people are very somber. No, everything is still in color. The breeze is blowing, the children are out playing, the world kept revolving. A good friend said to me, 'Paul, the troops aren't coming. We are the troops.' She might as well have kicked me. It's like I'm curled up in a fetal position in the corner saying, 'Well, when the economy changes' or 'After those people pay me back,' I'll be happy then. I'll be okay. When my friend said, 'The troops aren't coming,' I realized the only way out of this was to stand up, to get up and to go do something. To take my life back and live on purpose."

I check my digital recorder to make sure I'm getting all this. I'm not sure I've even been interviewing Dr. Paul. His mind seems to jump to the answers before I can ask the questions.

"There's a line from the movie *The Shawshank Redemption*," he says just before I leave. " 'Get busy living or get busy dying.' What if you were to choose? Intentionally. Steer in that direction." Dr. Paul laughs and opens his hands. "I don't know if that answers your question. I've got a Ph.D., Elizabeth. That stands for 'doctor of philosophy.' So I like to philosophize a lot. If you put a nickel in me, I'll run forever."

As I drive home, that line from the movie — *Get busy living or get busy dying* — makes me think of Alec Unsicker's family, who are so actively in the *get busy living* camp. My family is like that too.

Shortly after I was rescued, my family was invited to spend a week in the Dominican Republic at a resort called "Casa de Campo" — probably the nicest resort I have ever been to. We went deep-sea fishing, and all of us got seasick and puked our guts up over the side of the boat. (No, we didn't catch anything.) We went horseback riding on the beach on retired polo horses. We stayed in someone's home, and they had a butler and maids to prepare all the meals and do all the cleaning. Along with the house and staff, there were two golf carts assigned to us to get around in.

The whole trip was highly memorable, but the most memorable part for me and my brothers was the golf carts. I still get teased about this today. Maybe it was because I was approaching my sixteenth birthday and would soon be getting my driver's license or simply because I had never driven a golf cart before, but my brothers and I spent more time in the golf carts than at the beach or pool. On one of the sunshine-filled days, my brother Andrew and I switched carts partway through our driving adventure. When we finally decided to go back, my cart wasn't running quite as smoothly. I think maybe the batteries were running low or the fuel tank was almost empty. For whatever reason, I thought I had switched the cart into reverse, but I hadn't. I slammed my foot down on the accelerator (we may or may not have been racing back), and what do you know — I ran straight into a rock wall.

Andrew and I hurried back to the house

we were staying at and pretended that we hadn't done anything wrong, even though there was some damage to the front of the cart. Apparently they have a lot of security cameras set up at the resort, because less than ten minutes later, resort security guards showed up and started questioning my parents about the damage to the golf cart. And then they questioned Andrew because that was the cart he had been driving before we switched. It looked like Andrew was going to be in trouble, especially since he was really too young to drive the carts around.

But it was my fault, and I needed to take responsibility. I gathered my courage and said, "I'm sorry. It was me who crashed the cart. I thought I had put it in reverse, but I had it in natural, so instead of going backwards, I crashed into the stone wall."

My parents looked at me for a minute and then they started laughing, "I didn't know that you could put a cart in natural. Do you mean you put it in *neutral*?"

Natural, neutral, who cares? I was trying to take responsibility for what I had done and make sure my brother wasn't in trouble for my actions. The accident was soon forgotten, but even to this day, I am still given a hard time for saying "natural."

Whenever my brothers are in the car with me now and I get distracted for a second, they will slip the car into neutral and then when I press the accelerator, the engine just revs. Then they laugh and say, "Ha-ha! Look, Elizabeth, the car is in natural."

This is just a silly and slightly obnoxious experience — a slight detour from the topic — but for better or worse, it still makes me laugh. I suppose that when I tell this story to my kids someday, I'll spin it as a teachable moment — how we need to take responsibility for our actions or whatever — but the real point is that I learned from it. These are the moments that make up a life. And it's in the context of life as a whole that we learn from any experience, no matter how silly it is. Or how devastating.

Anne Morrow Lindbergh wrote in *Gift from the Sea:* "I do not believe that sheer suffering teaches. If suffering alone taught, all the world would be wise, since everyone suffers. To suffering must be added mourning, understanding, patience, love, openness, and the willingness to remain vulnerable."

Winding down the mountain road on my way home from the Unsicker's home, it strikes me that all these conversations are beginning to come together in the most unexpected ways. I feel privileged to be part of it all. I think of what the Unsickers have found in New Zealand, what Dr. Paul found on the way out of bankruptcy court, and what my parents knew when they held me in their arms after being called again and again to look at the remains of murdered girls who never made it home.

Sometimes we just need to ask ourselves: If today were my last day, would I be happy with how I lived it?

Was today worth living over again?

What am I going to do differently tomorrow?

What am I doing to "live on purpose"?

12
THE MYTH VERSUS THE REALITY OF HAPPILY EVER AFTER

Happiness is letting go of what you think your life is supposed to look like and celebrating it for everything that it is.

— MANDY HALE

Chloé is the embodiment of my "happily ever after." The moment she and I arrive at my parents' home, she beelines it straight to the dress-up box, where she proceeds to take off all her clothes, drape a necklace of plastic beads around her neck, and find the plastic high-heeled "oosh" shoes. My dad comes to give her a big hug and a kiss, but she objects. She loves hugs and kisses but doesn't like anyone getting in the way of what she wants to do at any given moment.

There's something extra special about my dad. Maybe it's the twinkle in his eye when he first sees you, or the extra squeeze he gives in his hugs. There's not a hard edge about him, but he's not a pushover. He's strong enough to hold the line, and he'd do anything for his kids. There's just something there that always makes you know that he loves you. We sit down across from each other. Chloé, of course, is prancing around in her plastic high heels, continually checking in on everyone to make sure she is not missing out on anything fun or interesting.

"Dad, do you believe in happily ever after?"

"You bet I do," he says. "I'll never forget the day you were rescued. I had returned to our home with the rest of the kids while you and Mom went to the hospital to be checked out. Well, there was an absolute sea of media on our street. It was so packed, you couldn't see the ground. The news reporters were all motioning to me to come out and make a comment. As I walked down the front stairs outside our home, I couldn't help but think of all the parents we had met during the past nine months who had children missing, and how they would give anything to have their child come home. I almost felt guilty. How were we so lucky to have you come home?"

"Did that day start out any different from any other?"

"No, it didn't. It was already stressful, because one of my brothers had made a

354

derogatory comment to the news, and it had been printed on the front page of the newspaper. It was supposed to be an 'off-the-record' comment, but he really should have known better because he worked in the media himself, and there is no such thing as an 'off-the-record' comment. Anyway, we got a phone call. Mom answered it, and it was Detective Cordon Parks. He asked to speak with me. When I answered, he told me I needed to come as quickly as I could down to the Sandy police station and that was all.

"Your mom didn't come with me. We didn't know what they'd called us for, but we always tried to not get our hopes up too high, because it was always so devastating when it wasn't you. When it was just some bones or a burned body, we were always so down. We had to protect ourselves by not allowing ourselves to be too hopeful anytime the police called. On the way down there, our family friend and PR guy Chris Thomas called and asked where I was. I was supposed to be at a press conference. I told him I had been asked to come as quickly as possible down to the police station. I actually thought maybe I was going to identify a body. Chris hung up and then called me back a few minutes later. He had a friend that worked in the Sandy police station who told him, 'They think they found Elizabeth.' Chris relayed the message to me. I'm not sure if it was nerves or the fact that all those buildings look the same, but I was having a hard time actually finding the station. Someone in the parking lot said, 'Mr. Smart, you're looking for the police station, and it's just on the other side.'

"When I walked in the front door, I was surprised to find about twelve police officers standing at attention. When I walked by them, they all said something like, 'God bless you,' 'I hope everything works out,' 'Good luck,' et cetera. When I got to the end of the hallway, I turned right, and there was Detective Parks waiting. He said, 'I think we found Elizabeth. Alive.' At that point, I was standing outside of a yellow door that had a small window with the metal wire crisscrossing through the glass. When I opened the door, I saw a young woman sitting there with her arms folded. Her hair was braided, and her face was badly sunburned and swollen. It was hard to reconcile the fact that this was you and that you had physically changed so much in only nine months. I remember you didn't react until I ran up to you, gave you a hug, held you back, and said, 'Elizabeth, is it really you?' That really was the beginning of our happily ever after."

My dad's memory and my memory of that day are similar and yet completely different. For me, my moment of knowing everything was going to be okay was him hugging me, but what was his moment? I ask, "Dad, at what point did you finally breathe again?"

"I think it was when we finally got you home. It was like we could finally be a family again and find some happiness. Find the relationships that we used to have."

"Did you worry that we wouldn't?"

"Once you were found, no, but I didn't want you to relive the whole nightmare. I just felt, *When does this crap leave center stage? And when can we resume our old normal?*"

"So, Dad, what do you think of happily ever after?"

"I think life is full of challenges," he says, "just like with 'Cinderella,' where things are happy, and the rescue has happened, and it says happily ever after, which is supposed to indicate that life is just a bowl full of cherries after. Life is full of challenges. So is life happy? Absolutely. Forever? No."

Chloé stomps over in her plastic high heels with a grape in one hand and a piece of bread in the other. She pats my knee, saying, "Mama, Mama, Mama." I pull her into my arms, fully aware that I am living my happily ever after. Now is our moment.

"My name is Inigo Montoya. You killed my father. Prepare to die." These are perhaps the most memorable lines in *The Princess Bride*. (Speaking of fairy tales that have their share of thorny patches.) Montoya spends twenty-plus years of his life in pursuit of the six-fingered man who killed his father. He's driven by revenge to become a master swordsman, an assassin. Due to Montoya's thirst for revenge, he misses so much of life. Ultimately, he does get his revenge upon the six-fingered man and rides away with his friends to the unknown future. The actor who played Montoya is Mandy Patinkin.

Mandy does have some similarities to his character in *The Princess Bride*. He has become a master of his trade: film, theater, television, singing — he's what you would call the "whole package." He sings, duels, and dances onstage and in the movies and performs heart surgery and fights terrorism on TV, but it's everything he is in real life that made me want to ask him about the concepts of hope and happily ever after. Mandy is also passionate about the things that are important to him. He cares deeply for his family, and he's overcome huge obstacles in his life, including a degenerative eye disease that required two corneal transplants. In 2004, he was diagnosed with prostate cancer, and in 2005, he and his son celebrated his first year of survivorship with a 265-mile bike ride for charity, the Arava Institute Hazon Israel Ride, the purpose of which is "Cycling for Peace, Partnership & Environmental Protection."

His presence is so big and joyful, most people don't know about the dark times he's gone through. And because he does good very quietly, most people aren't aware that Mandy is a huge humanitarian who has spent countless hours working with refugees. He carried people ashore in Greece as they were trying to escape the terrors of their native country.

I was very nervous to approach Mandy, even though we were sitting right next to each other at dinner. I didn't want to be one of "those" people who somehow seem to suck all the energy out of you, but I finally decided I was going to talk to him. I figured, *What's the worst that could happen? He doesn't answer or asks not to be bothered or moves away?* That would have surprised me; he didn't strike me as one of those celebrities who reacts that way. As I debated when and how best to ask him for an interview, I watched him interact with the other people sitting at the table. Polite, charming, and willing to speak to everyone who asked him questions. He, in my mind, is what a celebrity is. Not me. But when he got up to speak, he surprised me by talking quite passionately about me and about the mission of young people in the world.

When he sat back down, I mustered the courage to say, "Mandy, I'm working on a book about hope and healing. Do you think I could talk about it with you sometime in the future?"

"I would be happy to talk with you, Elizabeth," he said. "Anything to help you." And he smiled that *Princess Bride* smile.

So much for worrying about rejection. Mandy couldn't have been nicer. We arranged a phone interview.

When the day finally arrives, I dial Mandy's number, and Mandy quickly answers.

"How are you doing?" he asks me before I can ask him.

"Fine, thank you. How are you? Is this still an okay time to talk?"

"I'm driving to my place in the country," he says. "Do you mind if I put you on speaker?"

Of course I don't mind. I'm just happy to be talking to him, taking in this bighearted energy he gives off. "You are so busy; you perform in all areas of acting. Why is it important to you to then add to your load and engage in humanitarian work?"

"I've always tried to participate in humanitarian causes," he tells me, "particularly in the Middle East. I hope in optimism, and in my heart, I know that one day things will shift for the better. It is difficult, but in the meantime, I follow the precepts of my religion, which is *Tikkun Olam* — which means 'to repair the world.' It's our privilege and duty as citizens of this world to speak for those who have no voice. That's my job as a human being."

His religion, I've read, is what he calls "JewBu"; he's Jewish "with a dash of Buddhist belief." I make a note to research *Tikkun Olam,* but just Mandy's definition of it — to repair the world — makes me think of Angeline and Alec and all the people who've demonstrated an amazing ability to translate their hope into action that helps others.

"Mandy, when your cancer was first in remission and you took a 265-mile charity bike ride — I just wonder what that was for you. Was it, in some way, to prove to yourself that you were bigger than cancer?"

"I take hikes in a place where there's this mountaintop and there's a cliff over a beautiful lake. I went right before I took that bicycle trip and before I had the cancer operation. I went to that spot on that lake, and I looked out at this beautiful place where I often go to just say my prayers and think. I said, 'I'm coming back here. I'm coming back here after this surgery and after I do this bike ride, and I'm going to show you, Mr. Lake, that I'm good. I'm in good shape. I'll see you later.' I went and I did that bike ride to do exactly what you said: to prove to myself that I have conquered the struggle of fear with cancer and I've gone on to live my life, to ride with my son three hundred miles starting in Jerusalem on a bicycle with all these other people and be alive and do one of the most physically strenuous things I have ever attempted in my life. I did that to spite my own fear. Fear of this word *cancer* that, in that particular case, was a cancer that was supposedly interfering with my body.

"We are always in the situation to fight this fear," Mandy says. "Fear is the biggest thing that we're all dealing with. I personally get most frightened when I feel I'm wasting that time. Or if I have a conflict with a loved one or a friend or a family member or colleague. It pains me a great deal when there's a conflict because it's so hard to be in those situations, and I know I can't fix anything, but I want to do the best I can. Sometimes that just means letting the conflict stay there and trust it'll work itself out. Sometimes it means that there are things that I can do or say to help make the world better or the situation better with somebody I care deeply about."

"But given all the opportunities and conflicts, how do you balance your time?"

"The thing that I'm learning and keep trying to improve — when I was younger, I felt I had to work, work, work. More, more, more, more. I never scheduled time to recover, to rest, to reflect. I think that's an equally important part of my life as the work that I do or the time I spend with my family or my human rights work. Just to be by myself to rest, to sleep, to take walks. To think."

I know I should take a page from his book, take time to just be myself. Probably all of us need to do that. It's so easy to fill up our lives with stuff — meetings, agendas, schedules — it's hard to take the time we need to just be.

"I try not to live in the past but in the

moment," says Mandy. "As Buddhists often say, to live in this moment and to do the best I can from this moment forward. What I'm saying is, the darkness is what gets to the stars in the sky. The rain clouds give you the rainbows when the sun peeks behind them a little bit. You can't have one without the other. Sadness is one of the great gifts of life, because when you're sad, it lets you know when you're happy. If you never knew sadness, you'd never know how wonderful it was to be happy."

I guess I've never done the math on it that way, but I get what he's saying. Imagine the flatness of a life without highs and lows. Not that I wish those lowest lows on myself or anyone else, but I might be willing to concede that there is some beauty in the ugliest ordeals life has to offer. There's a sister, shivering on the porch beside you. There's a cup of cool water. There's harp music at your deathbed. There's New Zealand. There's love.

"We take happiness for granted," Mandy says. "Happiness and joy and good fortune — like food, and breath, and sunshine, and rain, and human love — shouldn't be taken for granted. It should be celebrated and appreciated for how precious it is and how fragile it is."

"Mandy, do you believe in 'happily ever after'?"

"Yes," he says with certainty. "It's just making it. The happily ever after state, for me, is to feel alive. To feel 100 percent alive. To feel that I'm doing good works for my world, my community, my fellow man and woman. If I can do that to the best of my ability at any time, if I don't waste the privilege of this day, if I live it to the best of my capabilities, then I feel I am living my life as best as I can. I can't ask any more of myself. That's all. I'm on a constant journey where I'm looking for light. And you define that light to be whatever you want. I haven't found it yet. I won't quit until my life is over, but I keep trying to find the light."

When the phrase "happily ever after" is heard, images of Cinderella and her prince riding off in their coach, Darth Vader accepting the light and dying, and Harry Potter finally vanquishing Lord Voldemort appear. Throughout this whole process, interviewing people, recording the conversations, researching, contemplating, and finally writing, I feel that my own concept of "happily ever after" has evolved.

I started out thinking that it was the silly ending to a child's fairy tale, that anyone who believed in it was just kidding themselves. I figured, our lives will never be perfect, we will always have problems, so why live thinking that one day we will hit smooth waters forever? Then that changed to thinking that we can attain "happily ever after" in life; it's not that we don't have challenges or problems, but it's being grateful for the goodness that we do have in our lives and accepting the hard times as they come. And finally it morphed yet again: yes, that stage of living with a grateful heart and accepting our trials as they come still applies, but even more than that, we have moments of heaven, perfection, happily ever after, whatever you want to call it, but we have them when we are living at 100 percent, full of love and hope.

The day I was rescued was a "happily ever after" moment. The day I got married to my soul mate was another. The day my little Chloé Rose came into our lives is perhaps the culmination and happiest of all "happily ever afters." If only every moment since her birth was as perfect and happy.

Just the other day, when Matthew and I sat down to dinner, I strapped Chloé into her high chair and turned my back for only a second. Matthew looked at her and said, "I think she has something stuck up her nose." We both jumped up and rushed over to her side to see what was shoved up her nose. I had introduced her to pomegranates earlier that day, and she loved them, but that perhaps wasn't the wisest food choice for a curious toddler. Still, considering all she usually wanted were Cheetos and Capri Sun juice pouches, I was delighted that she was excited about something fresh and healthy.

But sure enough, when we shined our phone lights up her nose, there lodged far out of her fingers' reach — and most certainly out of ours — was a pomegranate seed. I panicked, but Matthew remained calm.

"Run upstairs and get tweezers," he said.

I dashed up, grabbed the tweezers, and ran back down. By this time, Chloé was screaming her little lungs out. I did my best to hold her down while Matthew attempted to fish the seed out with the tweezers. Let's fast-forward past the drama and just say it didn't work. I was still frantic, trying to call my parents, her pediatrician, everyone I could think of, and no one was answering the phone.

Finally Matthew looked around in desperation and spotted his straw sticking out of the drink he was having with dinner. I was one step ahead of him. As soon as I saw him looking at the straw, I knew what he was thinking. I grabbed the straw and passed it to him. He gently inserted it into a very unhappy Chloé's nose, and sucked in a little sip of air. It worked. The pomegranate seed was dislodged, and we sat down at the table, laughing our heads off. This is a silly, silly moment in retrospect, but in the moment, it seemed like a catastrophe. No matter what stage or walk of life we find ourselves in, that's *life.* Moments of happily ever after competing with complete disaster. It is up to us how we perceive and react to life events that are out of our control.

To someone who knows nothing about my past, I might appear to have a perfect life. In reality, I have perfect moments in a life that, through no fault of my own, got very complicated when I was very young. My mother's voice comes back to me again and again: "Elizabeth, what these people have done to you is terrible. There aren't words strong enough to describe how wicked and evil they are. They've stolen nine months of your life that you will never get back. The best punishment you could ever give them is to be *happy* — to move on and do exactly what you want." Which leads to the Big Question: What *do* I want?

"I am what I choose to become," Carl Jung said. So each of us must ask himself or herself:

What defines me?

What have I chosen to become so far?

And looking to the future, what will I choose to become tomorrow?

AFTERWORD

"My name is Elizabeth Smart, and I have some questions I'd like to ask you."

A security camera glares down at me from above the wide front door of an alleged serial rapist I am reporting on for *Crime Watch Daily*. Usually, it's the victim I'm interviewing. Not this time. When he heard that this man was comfortably enjoying house arrest at a particularly posh address in a large Midwestern city, the producer asked me if I would feel comfortable approaching him. All I needed to say was "Let's go."

Now the producer stands with a security guard and the camera crew just below the porch steps, rolling tape as I bang on the door, which the man inside does not open. I didn't really expect him to talk with me. I just wanted him to know that his dark secret is about to get some this-little-light-of-mine shined on it. My own experience taught me the power of the media. If my parents hadn't kept my story in that powerful spotlight, I most likely would not have survived. My goal as a special correspondent for *Crime Watch Daily* is to bring that same kind of attention to the stories of other victims and to help everyone realize that sexual assault, kidnapping, and abuse don't just happen on the wrong side of the tracks; they can happen anywhere. We can't afford to turn a blind eye to what is happening all around us. Survivors — and victims who are still struggling to survive — need hope. They need to know they are not alone.

I wouldn't be able to do all the traveling and speaking and advocacy that I do without a rock-steady partner like Matthew. It's hard to be gone so often, especially now that I have a beautiful little girl and am about to have another baby. I believe the work I do is important, but I'm always so glad to get home. I want to be a faithful and loving wife, a kind and patient mother, a strong advocate for victims of violent and sexual crimes, and I want to be someone whom, at the end of the day, I still like and respect. Maybe that's my personal happily ever after: a life that combines all those things, a life filled with hope, made sweet by my husband and children, cleansed by faith, driven by purpose, fueled by a drive to see justice served, and lit up with joy in even the little things.

As I move forward in my own life dealing with love, relationships, anger, and most of all with hope, I am continually reminded that we all face challenges, big and small. Sometimes they are laughable, but many times they are much more serious. Even heartbreaking. We each have a story to tell, and my story is not finished. I will continue to have trials and ups and downs, not least of which will be coming in April with baby number two. How have women survived childbirth for so many years? How have women and men survived parenthood in general?

As I finish the final draft of this book, I'm also thinking of you, the person my editor friend calls "We the Reader." I wonder about the circumstances that led you to this book, and I hope that in it you've found some answers, some help, some hope.

In the Gospel According to Matthew, Jesus gives his famous Sermon on the Mount. "Ask and it shall be given you," he says. "Seek and ye shall find." So I asked, and I sought, but as I upload the last of my interview files — long, thought-provoking conversations with my dad and Mandy — I'm left with another long hallway of doors to knock on. One of the many lessons I've learned in this process is that things aren't always what you assume they are. When you see a small sliver of someone's life — whether you read about someone in the paper or see them on TV or observe them through whatever filter they're holding up — you can be sure that there's a whole story there that you don't know. The Scottish theologian Ian Maclaren wrote, "Be kind, for everyone you meet is fighting a hard battle."

Every day, I hear of or meet with people who have so much to give, so much to teach, even if it's just the light they shine by living. I thought I would come to the end of this book and sum up all the answers I had wrangled. I certainly don't have all the answers, and I as I grow older, I recognize the truth in that old adage "The older I get, the more I realize how little I know." At the end of every journey, project, campaign, or trial, we can analyze our experience quite simply by asking ourselves these two questions:

What did I learn?

Was it worth it?

For me, I can honestly say I have learned so much, and yes, without a doubt, it has been worth it. God bless you in all that you currently face and all that lies before you.

CONTRIBUTORS

I hope you'll be moved to learn more about the remarkable people interviewed in this book. They're listed here in order of appearance, along with some of their books, organizations, and websites:

Ed and Lois Smart
  Bringing Elizabeth Home: A Journey of Faith and Hope
  The Elizabeth Smart Foundation
  www.elizabethsmartfoundation.org

Ann Romney
  In This Together: My Story
  Ann Romney Center for Neurologic Diseases
  http://give.brighamandwomens.org/stories/ann-romney-center-about

Bre Lasley
  Fight Like Girls

www.fightlikegirls.org

Mary Louise Zeller
Secrets of the Fountain of Youth
www.teamusa.org/usa-taekwondo/
athletes/MaryLouise-Zeller

Norma Bastidas
Running Home: A Journey to End Violence
http://mexicanrunningwild.blogspot.com

Fatima

Rebecca Covey
Bridle Up Hope: The Rachel Covey
Foundation
www.bridleuphope.org

Elder Richard G. Hinkley

Diane von Furstenberg
The Woman I Wanted to Be
Diane: A Signature Life
The Diller-von Furstenberg Family
Foundation
www.dvf.com/philanthropy

Mariatu Kamara
The Bite of the Mango

Lara Oles
LOPE: Lara Oles Para Equestrian
www.lope.org

Helen Golden

Angeline Jackson
Quality of Citizenship Jamaica
www.qcjm.org

Chris Williams
Let It Go: A True Story of Tragedy and Forgiveness
http://justletgomovie.com

Archbishop John C. Wester
Archdiocese of Sante Fe
www.archdiocesesantafe.org

Mike Schlappi
Shot Happens
http://mikeschlappi.com

Alec Unsicker
AJU Foundation
https://ajufoundation.com

Dr. Paul Jenkins
Pathological Positivity
http://pathologicalpositivity.com

Mandy Patinkin
www.mandypatinkin.org

ACKNOWLEDGMENTS

I'm deeply grateful to my family: Matthew, my wonderful husband, thank you for your support and faith in me. Chloé, whether you wanted to or not, you shared your mom with this project, and James, you were born right along with this book, but I hope you both know that you have all my love every day of your lives. I'm humbly grateful to all the contributors who agreed to be interviewed for this book. You opened your hearts and allowed me to ask questions that were sometimes difficult to answer. Your generosity and courage have inspired and set an example for me. Thank you, from the bottom of my heart. I'm blessed to work with a wonderful publishing team, beginning with the faith and advocacy of my agent, Kelly Crabb. Joni Rodgers, my stalwart Sherpa and friend throughout the writing process, helped me build the vehicle for my vision and opened my eyes to what I'm capable of on my own. With an open mind and big heart, my editor, Charles Spicer, gave me the freedom to explore this idea and stepped in with wise council when needed. He and the team at St. Martin's have done a beautiful job bringing it all together and guiding it into the hands of readers. Heartfelt thanks to you all.

ABOUT THE AUTHOR

Elizabeth Smart is an American activist, president of the Elizabeth Smart Foundation, and *New York Times* bestselling author of *My Story.* She first gained widespread attention at age fourteen when she was kidnapped from her home and rescued nine months later.